Citizen Linguistics in Language Resource Development (CLLRD 2020)

Marseille, France
11 – 16 May 2020

Editors:

James Fiumara
Christopher Cieri
Mark Liberman
Chris Callison-Burch

ISBN: 978-1-7138-1255-5

Printed from e-media with permission by:

Curran Associates, Inc.
57 Morehouse Lane
Red Hook, NY 12571

CURRAN ASSOCIATES INC. proceedings.com

Some format issues inherent in the e-media version may also appear in this print version.

Association for Computational Linguistics
209 N. Eighth Street
Stroudsburg, Pennsylvania 18360

Phone: 1-570-476-8006
Fax: 1-570-476-0860

acl@aclweb.org

Additional copies of this publication are available from:

Curran Associates, Inc.
57 Morehouse Lane
Red Hook, NY 12571 USA
Phone: 845-758-0400
Fax: 845-758-2633
Email: curran@proceedings.com
Web: www.proceedings.com

LREC 2020 Workshop
Language Resources and Evaluation Conference
11–16 May 2020

Citizen Linguistics in Language Resource Development (CLLRD 2020)

PROCEEDINGS

James Fiumara, Christopher Cieri, Mark Liberman,
Chris Callison-Burch (eds.)

Proceedings of the LREC 2020 Workshop
Citizen Linguistics in Language Resource Development
(CLLRD 2020)

Edited by: James Fiumara, Christopher Cieri, Mark Liberman, and Chris Callison-Burch

For more information:
European Language Resources Association (ELRA)
9 rue des Cordelières
75013, Paris
France
http://www.elra.info
Email: lrec@elda.org

Introduction

Welcome to the LREC2020 Workshop on Citizen Linguistics in Language Resource Development.

Notwithstanding advances in data collection and processing, language related research, education and technology development continue to suffer from inadequate supply of Language Resources. To supplement traditional LR development, which typically relies upon top down support from some government or private foundation, Citizen Linguistics (the Citizen Science of Language) changes the incentive model to attract a new workforce which in turn requires a different kind of workflow. Incentives to Citizen Linguists may include the opportunities to learn and develop new skills; to socialize, compete and earn status or recognition; to document their language and promote their culture and, most importantly, to contribute directly to research and indirectly to a greater cause or social good. By offering human contributors sustained access to appropriate opportunities, activities, and incentives, we can enhance LR development well beyond what traditional direct funding alone can produce. However, along with these new incentives and workflows come new challenges whose solutions are relevant even to expert (paid) annotation.

The goal of this hybrid workshop/tutorial is two-fold. First is to provide a forum for researchers and practitioners to explore and discuss the issues, advantages and challenges of using Citizen Linguistics as a method for the creation of language resources. Second is to introduce LanguageARC, a new Citizen Linguistics web portal for collecting language data and judgements.

Organizers:

Chris Callison-Burch, University of Pennsylvania, USA
Christopher Cieri, Linguistic Data Consortium, University of Pennsylvania, USA
James Fiumara, Linguistic Data Consortium, University of Pennsylvania, USA
Mark Liberman, Linguistic Data Consortium, University of Pennsylvania, USA

Program Committee:

Sonja Bosch, University of South Africa, South Africa
Chris Callison-Burch, University of Pennsylvania, USA
Nicoletta Calzolari, Institute for Computational Linguistics, Italy
Khalid Choukri, ELRA/ELDA, France
Christopher Cieri, Linguistic Data Consortium, University of Pennsylvania, USA
John Coleman, Oxford University, UK
Maxine Eskenazi, Carnegie Mellon University, USA
Karën Fort, Sorbonne Université, France
James Fiumara, Linguistic Data Consortium, University of Pennsylvania, USA
Mark Liberman, Linguistic Data Consortium, University of Pennsylvania, USA
Peter Patrick, University of Essex, UK
Massimo Poesio, Queen Mary University of London, UK
Stephanie Strassel, Linguistic Data Consortium, University of Pennsylvania, UK
Jennifer Tracey, Linguistic Data Consortium, University of Pennsylvania, UK

Invited Speaker:

John Coleman, Oxford University, UK

Table of Contents

LanguageARC: Developing Language Resources Through Citizen Linguistics
James Fiumara, Christopher Cieri, Jonathan Wright and Mark Liberman 1

Developing Language Resources with Citizen Linguistics in Austria – A Case Study
Barbara Heinisch 7

Objective Assessment of Subjective Tasks in Crowdsourcing Applications
Giannis Haralabopoulos, Myron Tsikandilakis, Mercedes Torres Torres and Derek McAuley . . . 15

Speaking Outside the Box: Exploring the Benefits of Unconstrained Input in Crowdsourcing and Citizen Science Platforms
Jon Chamberlain, Udo Kruschwitz and Massimo Poesio 26

Leveraging Non-Specialists for Accurate and Time Efficient AMR Annotation
Mary Martin, Cecilia Mauceri, Martha Palmer and Christoffer Heckman 35

The INCOMSLAV Platform: Experimental Website with Integrated Methods for Measuring Linguistic Distances and Asymmetries in Receptive Multilingualism
Irina Stenger, Klara Jagrova and Tania Avgustinova 40

Identifications of Speaker Ethnicity in South-East England: Multicultural London English as a Divisible Perceptual Variety
Amanda Cole 49

LanguageARC - a tutorial
Christopher Cieri and James Fiumara 58

Proceedings of the LREC 2020 Workshop "Citizen Linguistics in Language Resource Development", pages 1–6
Language Resources and Evaluation Conference (LREC 2020), Marseille, 11–16 May 2020

LanguageARC: Developing Language Resources Through Citizen Linguistics

James Fiumara, Christopher Cieri, Jonathan Wright, Mark Liberman
University of Pennsylvania, Linguistic Data Consortium
Philadelphia, PA USA
{jfiumara, ccieri, jdwright, my}@ldc.upenn.edu

Abstract

This paper introduces the citizen science platform, LanguageARC, developed within the NIEUW (Novel Incentives and Workflows) project supported by the National Science Foundation under Grant No. 1730377. LanguageARC is a community-oriented online platform bringing together researchers and "citizen linguists" with the shared goal of contributing to linguistic research and language technology development. Like other Citizen Science platforms and projects, LanguageARC harnesses the power and efforts of volunteers who are motivated by the incentives of contributing to science, learning and discovery, and belonging to a community dedicated to social improvement. Citizen linguists contribute language data and judgments by participating in research tasks such as classifying regional accents from audio clips, recording audio of picture descriptions and answering personality questionnaires to create baseline data for NLP research into autism and neurodegenerative conditions. Researchers can create projects on Language ARC without any coding or HTML required using our Project Builder Toolkit.

Keywords: citizen science, crowdsourcing, language resources, novel incentives

1. Introduction

Linguistic research and Human Language Technology (HLT) development have greatly benefited from the large amount of linguistic data that has been created and shared by data centers, governments and research groups around the globe. However, despite these efforts, the amount and variety of available Language Resources (LRs) falls far short of need. Current approaches to LR development are unlikely to solve the dearth of LRs due to both the overall amount of effort required and to the reliance on finite project-focused funding and collection. The Linguistic Data Consortium (LDC)'s NIEUW (Novel Incentives and Workflows) project supported by the National Science Foundation under Grant No. 1730377 was developed to address these issues by utilizing novel incentives and workflows to collect a variety of linguistic data and annotations and make that data widely available to the research community.

2. Language Resources

Human language technologies, linguistic research and language pedagogy all rely heavily on a variety of LRs. Despite the ongoing efforts of data centers such as the LDC[1], European Language Resources Association (ELRA)[2], Chinese LDC[3], LDC for Indian Languages[4] and the Southern African Centre for Digital Language Resources (SADiLaR)[5], multinational projects such as CLARIN[6] and numerous national and regional corpus creation efforts, the public availability of language resources is only a fraction of what is truly needed for linguistic research and HLT development. One predominant factor is simply that there is a large number of languages in the world; over 7000 by some counts (Eberhard, Simons & Fennig 2019). In addition, the number of resources required to develop minimally necessary technologies in any given language is as much as two dozen (Krauwer 1998, Binnenpoorte, et al. 2002, Krauwer 2003). Another contributing issue is that new language resource production frequently does not result in maximum coverage of languages and resources types, but rather tends to increase the size of existing LRs (Cieri 2017).

In summary, the current approaches to developing LRs required for research and HLT development insufficiently address the problem of lack of language resources. If we hope to rectify the scarcity and imbalance of available resources, new methods of data collection and annotation are required.

3. Novel Approaches to LR Creation

A primary reason that current approaches of LR creation are insufficient is that they tend to rely on finite funding resources for a problem that is multiple orders of magnitude greater. While we are not proposing to replace traditional methods of funding LR development, a promising alternative or supplement is to harness renewable resources that rely on incentives other than monetary. Social media, citizen science and games with a purpose (GWAP) have demonstrated that humans are willing to volunteer vast stores of effort given appropriate opportunities and incentives, which include: competition, entertainment, desire to demonstrate expertise, learning and discovery, the desire to contribute to science or a larger social good and participating in a community. Successful examples include the now defunct The Great Language Game (Skirgård, Roberts, & Yencken 2017) which collected tens of millions of language ID judgments and the citizen science platform, Zooniverse[7], which has solicited hundreds of millions of contributions from approximately two million volunteers.

Following similar incentive models, we have identified three overlapping communities that seem the most promising for these efforts: game players, citizen scientists and language students and teachers. Under the NIEUW project, we are creating community platforms for each of

[1] https://www.ldc.upenn.edu
[2] http://www.elra.info
[3] http://www.chineseldc.org
[4] http://www.ldcil.org
[5] https://sadilar.org
[6] https ://www.clarin.eu
[7] https://www.zooniverse.org

these three communities. We have completed online platforms for game players and citizen linguists and a platform designed for Linguistics students and teachers is currently in development.

Our games portal, LingoBoingo[8], currently includes nine language games developed by LDC and colleagues at University of Pennsylvania's Department of Computer and Information Science, the University of Essex, Queen Mary University of London, Sorbonne Université, Loria (the Lorraine Laboratory of Research in Computing and its Applications), Inria (the French National Institute for Computer Science and Applied Mathematics), and the Université de Montpellier. Lovers of language, grammar and literature can test their knowledge, compete against other players and earn high scores in a variety of linguistic games. Among these nine games is LDC's own Name That Language![9] game which is inspired by The Great Language Game and has already collected nearly 450,000 judgments since October 2018.

However, the bulk of the NIEUW effort has been dedicated to building our citizen science platform, LanguageARC[10].

4. Citizen Linguistics

Contributions to scientific research by the public have a long history, e.g. Edmund Halley soliciting assistance from the public to map solar eclipses (Pasachoff, 1999) and the annual Christmas Bird Count organized by the Audubon Society which started in 1900 (Root, 1988). The advent of the internet, smartphones and social media have only increased the public's ability and incentives to contribute to scientific research endeavors. Following this history, LanguageARC (**A**nalysis **R**esearch **C**ommunity) is a citizen science platform and community dedicated to language; henceforth, "citizen linguistics" and "citizen linguists."

Figure 1: Citizen Linguist portal, LanguageARC.

4.1 LanguageARC Overview

LanguageARC hosts multiple *projects* to which citizen linguists can contribute. A project may contain one or multiple *tasks* and each task is composed of a discrete activity that can be applied to multiple *items* or input data.

For example, the project *From Cockney to the Queen* seeks to identify and understand how people speak across London and Southwest England in relation to various demographics. One task asks contributors to listen to an audio clip and identify the region which the speaker likely comes from, while another task asks contributors to record themselves discussing their own experiences and understandings of language differences across geographic areas. In these tasks, the *items* include audio clips and maps and the contributions include speech recordings and judgments made via button selections.

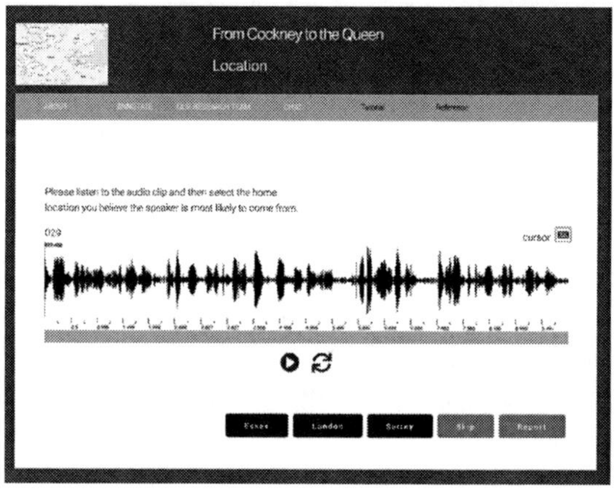

Figure 2: LanguageARC task

Individuals can become a member of the LanguageARC community by providing as little as login ID and email address used for verification purposes, although the registration form also provides a space to collect optional demographic information such as gender, date of birth, languages spoken and geographic regions where one has lived. Once someone joins the LanguageARC community they can participate in any public project on the platform which can be found on the Project menu page (Fig. 3).

LanguageARC also allows the option for private projects which can be accessed by invitation only (though one is still required to join LanguageARC in order to access private projects). Private projects will only be visible to those who have been invited and added to the project. This gives researchers the ability to create a task for a restricted group of contributors such as members of their lab, postdocs or students in one of their courses.

[8] https://lingoboingo.org

[9] https://namethatlanguage.org

[10] https://languagearc.org

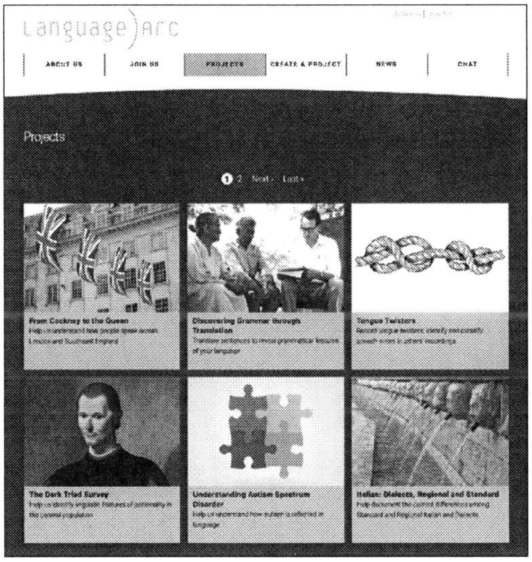

Figure 3: LanguageARC Project menu

Future updates to the project menu page will include search and filter options allowing the ability to search by keyword and filter by categories such as date added, alphabetical by name, the target language of the project and which projects need the most assistance from the community.

4.2 LanguageARC Structure

LanguageARC presents each project by its title, a call to action subtitle, a project image and a brief project description in the form of a pitch. Other project features include a section to highlight the members of the research team and a place for logos and links to the research team's supporting organizations and sponsors. Each project also has the option to have their own project message boards to support community building and provide a place for the citizen linguists to interact with the researchers and each other. Each individual task within a project may have its own title, call to action, task image and message as well as tutorials and reference guides to provide background and instructional materials to the citizen linguists.

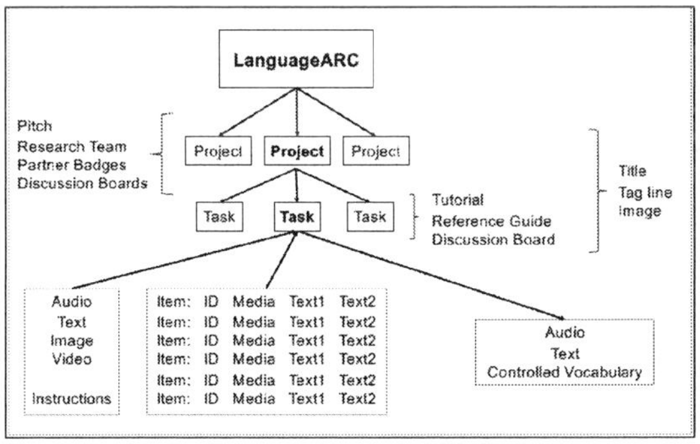

Figure 4: Project structure flow chart

Figure 4 shows the overall structure of LanguageARC described above. The figure also outlines the basic structure of tasks which consist of an *input* (audio, text, video, image), a *tool* which allows contributor interaction with the input, and an *output* (audio, text, controlled vocabulary).

4.3 Toolkit and Project Builder

LanguageARC was created using a modified version of a toolkit that the LDC has built and used to create millions of annotations across more than 100 language resource projects over the past decade. The toolkit has been adapted, modified and extended to make it portable to new environments including on the web. The toolkit has also been made open source and is capable of being deployed to a laptop and taken into the field where there may be no internet access. The modified toolkit source code will be made available on GitHub or similar repository and may be used by researchers outside of the LanguageARC platform. In order to make LanguageARC accessible to as wide a group of researchers as possible, we have created a Project Builder that allows users with no coding or software development experience to easily create and deploy annotation and collection tasks by uploading appropriately formatted data and answering a number of questions presented within a series of templates.

The Project Builder provides a series of ordered templates that takes the creator step-by-step through the build process from general information (e.g., project name, description) to specific task details (e.g., input data, tool features).

Figure 5: Project Builder menu

In Step 1 you can create a new project or select an already existing project to update. After the basic project information is created, Step 2 allows you to create a new annotation task or select a current task for updating. Each project must have at least one task, but may have multiple tasks within a single project. Task tutorials and reference guides can also be created with markup language and can include images, videos and audio clips.

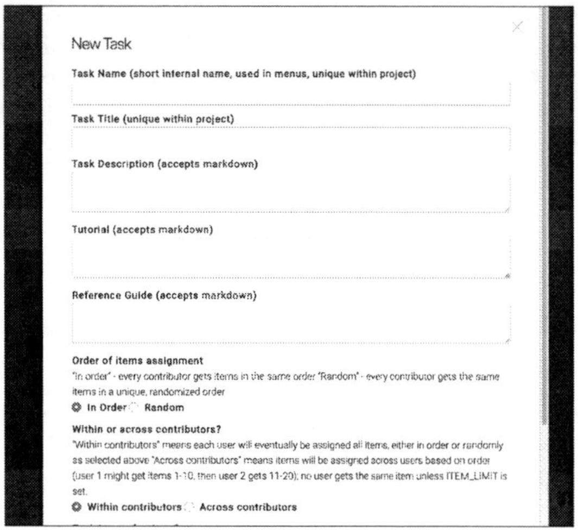

Figure 6: Task creation template

Step 3 in the Project Builder is to upload your input data (image, audio, video or text) and a tab delimited manifest file that orders and labels the input data. Finally, the last step in the Project Builder is to create the tool itself.

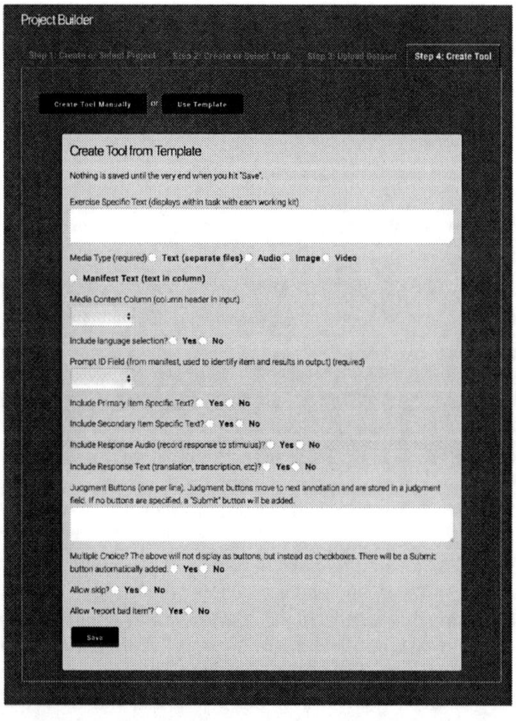

Figure 7: Tool builder template

Building the tool is also accomplished by answering a series of questions that tells the software what the input data is, which relevant data columns to select in the manifest, and what type of annotation interactions and outputs are desired.

Currently, the Project Builder is only available internally to LDC researchers. In the near future, the ability to create Projects will be available to the wider research community. Additional interactive instructions and guidelines for building projects will be included on the website. There will be a process where built projects will need to be approved prior to being made publically available.

Overall, the Project Builder has been designed so that with no coding knowledge required and just a small amount of prep work to prepare input data, projects and tasks can be created in as little as one hour or less.

5. Projects on LanguageARC

LanguageARC currently hosts a small number of projects created by the LDC and colleagues. Projects will be added on an ongoing basis and the number should grow exponentially once the Project Builder is made available to the larger research community. We will describe a few of the projects below to provide more in depth examples of the kinds of collection and annotation projects LanguageARC is capable of supporting.

5.1 From Cockney to the Queen

The project *From Cockney to the Queen* was developed in collaboration with researchers from the Linguistics department at the University of Essex. The goal of the project is to collect data and judgments to support sociolinguistic research into perceptions of regional accents in London and Southeast England. The project contains seven different tasks that ask citizen linguists to classify accents based on a variety of demographic information such as ethnicity, social class and geographic location.

Figure 8: Speech recording task

Additional tasks allow contributors to provide their own experiences and definitions of these demographic features by uploading audio recordings. By using the audio player and audio recording widgets in the Project Builder Toolkit organized around multiple demographic features (ethnicity, social class and location), *From Cockney to the Queen* can collect large amounts of both judgments about accents and raw linguistic data.

5.2 Discovering Grammar Through Translation

The project, *Discovering Grammar Through Translation,* elicits translations from contributors to create bilingual data in English and the native language of the citizen linguist. Using the Elicitation Corpus created at Carnegie Mellon University's Language Technologies Institute,[11] this translation task includes contextual information to elicit translations that reveal grammatical features of languages such as gender, number and tense.

Figure 9: Translation task

The translation task requires that the contributor select a language for the task. The language selection box presents a scrollable list of languages containing all of the > 61,000 names used to refer to the world's 7400 languages with their ISO Language Code in parentheses. A source sentence for translation is provided along with contextual information to guide the translation. For example:

Source: Michael was greeting Patricia.
Context: The speaker asserts this sentence to be true.

Translations are entered into a text box and can be edited until the submit button is selected.

5.3 Clinical NLP Projects

The application of natural language processing to brain disorders such as autism spectrum disorder and frontotemporal degenerative disorders has shown great promise in increasing scientific understanding and clinical diagnosis (Cho et al. 2019, Parish-Morris et al. 2017). In order to identify and study the linguistic patterns and correlates of clinical conditions, researchers need extensive data from the general population to serve as a baseline for psychometric norming. LanguageARC can help collect these baseline datasets by creating tasks that mimic activities used in clinical settings allowing analysis of similar data across those with known clinical disorders and the general population.

5.3.1 Understanding Autism Spectrum Disorder

The Linguistic Data Consortium and the Center for Autism Research at Children's Hospital of Philadelphia[12] have been collaborating to develop LRs and apply human language technologies to the study of autism spectrum disorder (Parish-Morris et al. 2016).

The LanguageARC project *Understanding Autism Spectrum Disorder* asks contributors to complete two related tasks.

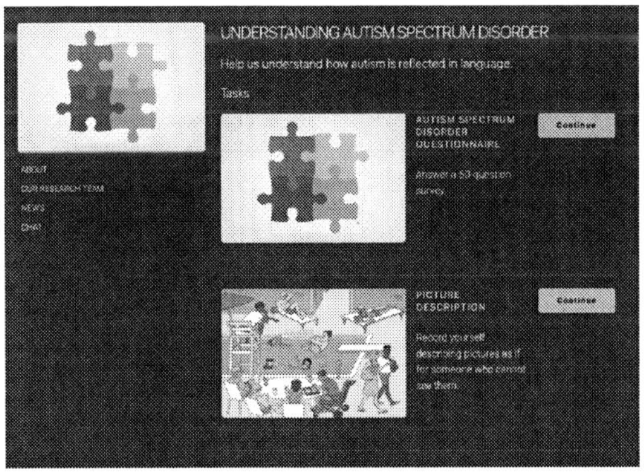

Figure 10: Understanding Autism Spectrum Disorder tasks

The first task asks the citizen linguist to answer the 50-questions Autism Quotient (AC) survey developed by the Autism Research Centre at Cambridge University.[13] While the AQ elicits self-report of traits associated with Autism Spectrum Disorders, LanguageARC's use of the instrument is not for purposes of individual diagnosis and no results are returned to contributors.

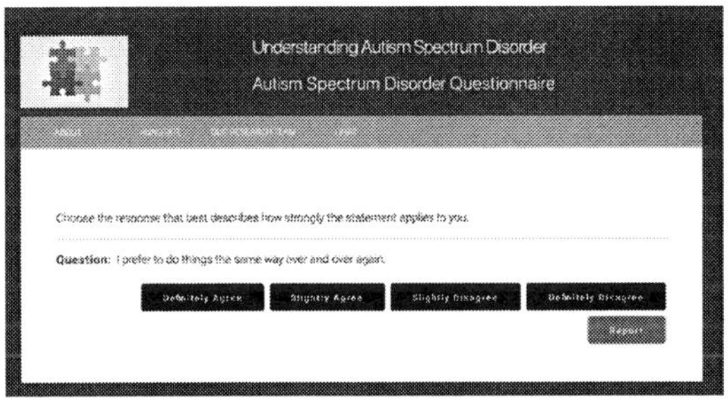

Figure 11: Questionnaire task

A second task asks contributors to complete a series of picture descriptions via an audio recording tool. Picture description tasks are commonly used in clinical settings. The combination of the two tasks allows the project to collect AQ results and corresponding linguistic data via the picture description from the overall general population allowing the creation of a large baseline dataset to assist in clinical research.

[11] https://www.lti.cs.cmu.edu

[12] https://www.centerforautismresearch.org

[13] https://www.autismresearchcentre.com

It should be repeated that these tasks designed for citizen linguists are not intended to provide diagnosis and do not provide test scores or feedback to the contributor.

5.3.2 The Dark Triad Survey

The Dark Triad Survey is a questionnaire used by psychologists to measure the personality traits of narcissism, psychopathy and Machiavellianism. As with the autism spectrum survey, this task is not intended as diagnostic and no scores are reported to the citizen linguist participants.

Similar to *Understanding Autism Spectrum Disorder*, the *Dark Triad Survey* project presents two tasks to the citizen linguist. The first is a 27-question survey used to measure dark triad personality traits and the second is a series of picture description tasks. The results will be aggregated with those of the other contributors to show how the whole population performs on these language tasks and provide data for investigating linguistic markers of personality type.

6. Project Reports and Recruitment

Project managers can access the output data collected through their tasks by selecting the report option within their user dashboard. Reports are tab delimited and contain details of every annotation made by users within the task including ID# to identify the project, task, and tool (which change if you update the task); a user ID and geographic location; the date and time of the annotation; and the content of the annotation if it is text entry or controlled vocabulary selections (i.e., button selections). For user annotations in audio format (such as picture description audio recordings) a separate download function is currently being developed.

LanguageARC requires the recruitment of two kinds of contributors: researchers and volunteer contributors. In this early phase of the project, LDC is both creating its own research projects and working with external colleagues to populate the portal with research projects. LDC has also been promoting LanguageARC in other venues likely to reach language researchers such as LREC and LinguistList. Building and sustaining a community of volunteer "citizen linguists" is perhaps an even bigger challenge. LDC is working to build its volunteer community by publicizing LanguageARC through a variety of venues and social media sites including advertising on Facebook and Twitter and promoting through related citizen science communities such as SciStarter.

7. Conclusion

LanguageARC uses novel incentives to address the limitations of current approaches to developing LRs that rely on project-constrained funding. By appealing to the motivations of citizen science, LanguageARC seeks to develop a community of citizen linguists and researchers working toward common goals. The powerful but easy-to-use Project Builder Toolkit and user friendly participant interface allows the creation of a wide variety of data collection and annotation tasks suitable for non-expert contributors. The data that results from projects and tasks developed with NSF funds will be made freely available to the research community.

8. Acknowledgments

The authors would like to acknowledge the support of the National Science Foundation under Grant No. 1730377.

9. Bibliographical References

Binnenpoorte, Diana, Catia Cucchiarini, Elisabeth D'Halleweyn, Janienke Sturm and Folkert de Vriend (2002) Towards a roadmap for Human Language Technologies: Dutch-Flemish experience in Proceedings of the workshop "Towards a Roadmap for Multimodal Language Resources and Evaluation" at LREC 2002, Las Palmas, Canary Islands, June.

Cho, Sunghye, Mark Liberman, Neville Ryant, Meredith Cola, Robert T. Schultz, Julia Parish-Morris (2019) Automatic detection of Autism Spectrum Disorder in children using acoustic and text features from brief natural conversations. Interspeech: 20th Annual Conference of the International Speech Communication Association Graz, September 15-19, 2019.

Cieri, C. (2017) Addressing the Language Resource Gap through Alternative Incentives, Workforces and Workflows, Keynote Speech at the 8th Language & Technology Conference, November 17-19, Poznań, Poland.

Eberhard, David M., Gary F. Simons, and Charles D. Fennig (eds.). 2019. Ethnologue: Languages of the World. Twenty-second edition. Dallas, Texas: SIL International. http://www.ethnologue.com.

Krauwer, Steven (1998) ELSNET and ELRA: Common past, common future, ELRA Newsletter, Vol. 3:2, May.

Krauwer, Steven (2003) The Basic Language Resource Kit (BLARK) as the First Milestone for the Language Resources Roadmap, in International Workshop Speech and Computer (SPECOM-2003).

Pasachoff, J. M. (1999). "Halley as an eclipse pioneer: his maps and observations of the total solar eclipses of 1715 and 1724," Journal of Astronomical History and Heritage, vol. 2, no. 1, pp. 39-54.

Parish-Morris, Julia, Mark Liberman, Christopher Cieri, John Herrington, Benjamin Yerys, Leila Batman, Joseph Donaher, Emily Ferguson, Juhi Pandey, Robert Schultz Linguistic Camouflage in Girls with Autism Spectrum Disorder. *Molecular Autism,* September 30, 2017

Parish-Morris, Julia, Christopher Cieri, Mark Liberman, Leila Bateman, Emily Ferguson, Robert T. Schultz (2016). Building Language Resources for Exploring Autism Spectrum Disorders. LREC: 10th Edition of the Language Resources and Evaluation Conference Portoroz, May 23-28, 2016.

Strötgen, J. and Gertz, M. (2012). Temporal tagging on different domains: Challenges, strategies, and gold standards. In Nicoletta Calzolari (Conference Chair), et al., editors, Proceedings of the Eight International Conference on Language Resources and Evaluation (LREC'12), pages 3746–3753, Istanbul, Turkey, may. European Language Resource Association (ELRA).

Proceedings of the LREC 2020 Workshop "Citizen Linguistics in Language Resource Development", pages 7–14
Language Resources and Evaluation Conference (LREC 2020), Marseille, 11–16 May 2020

Developing Language Resources with Citizen Linguistics in Austria – A Case Study

Barbara Heinisch
Centre for Translation Studies, University of Vienna, Austria
Gymnasiumstraße 50, 1190 Vienna
barbara.heinisch@univie.ac.at

Abstract

Language resources are a major ingredient for the advancement of language technologies. Citizen linguistics can help to create language resources and annotate language resources, not only for the improvement of language technologies, such as machine translation but also for the advancement of linguistic research. The (language) resources covered in this article are a corpus related to the Question of the Month project strand, which was initially aimed at co-creation in citizen linguistics and a partially annotated database of pictures of written text in different languages found in the public sphere. The number of participants in these project strands differed significantly. Especially those activities that were related to data collection (and analysis) had a significantly higher number of contributions per participant. This especially held true for the activities with (prize) incentives. Nevertheless, the activities of the Question of the Month could reach a higher number of participants, even after the co-creation approach was no longer followed. In addition, the Question of the Month brought research gaps and new knowledge to light and challenged existing paradigms and practices. These are especially important for the advancement of scholarly research. Citizen linguistics can help gather and analyze linguistic data, including language resources, in a short period of time. Thus, it may help increase the access to and availability of language resources.

Keywords: Language varieties, citizen linguistics, language resource development

1. Introduction

The history of citizen linguistics in Austria looks back on a long tradition. Since citizen linguistics takes different forms, we may differentiate between citizens contributing to linguistic research that is coordinated and supervised by scholars, on the one hand, and so-called amateur linguists, on the other. Examples of activities by the latter are dictionaries compiled by people who are not trained lexicographers. This is because linguistics lends itself to the contribution by citizens since everybody uses language. This contribution goes beyond being a scholar's subject of investigation as speakers of a language (variety). It is rather about finding new research topics, data collection, data analysis or interpretation done by citizens according to scholarly principles.

1.1 History of Citizen Linguistics in Austria

Citizen linguistics in Austria dates back to the Habsburg Monarchy in the 19th century when it had a strong focus on the collection of linguistic data, especially of dialects. Two examples of these research initiatives in which citizens played an important role in collecting data from the actual speakers of dialects are the Dictionary of Bavarian Dialects in Austria (*Wörterbuch der bairischen Mundarten in Österreich*, WBÖ) and the Wenker Atlas.

In both cases, so-called amateur explorers were asked to empirically collect data of the local dialects. While the WBÖ was launched by two chancelleries in today's Germany and Austria, the Wenker-Atlas was initiated by Georg Wenker, who was a librarian in today's Germany.

1.1.1 Wörterbuch der bairischen Mundarten in Österreich (WBÖ)

The WBÖ was initiated with the aim to chart the Bavarian dialect region (*gesamtbairischen Dialektraum*) in a dialect dictionary. Since this endeavour was aimed at a comprehensive and systematic study of this dialect region, the scholars required help from volunteer data collectors who were recruited through newspaper announcements. The recruited explorers received written instructions for surveying the local population speaking the typical local dialect and collecting lexical data. Since then and over centuries, these data had been fed into the WBÖ dictionary (Stöckle, 2019; ÖAW-ACDH; WBÖ, 2020).

1.1.2 Wenker Atlas

The Wenker Atlas was aimed at finding the boundaries of dialects in the German Reich and at compiling the data in the *Sprachatlas des Deutschen Reichs* language atlas. To achieve the highest possible density of data collection points, local teachers served as explorers. They were tasked with the translation of the Wenker sentences that were written in standard German language into the local dialect. These data were then fed into the language atlas (Herrgen, 2010; DiWA, 2019).

In both cases, volunteers served as citizen linguists who collected data for linguistic research.

In the following section, the peculiarities of the Austrian variety of the German language are addressed to understand the background of the citizen linguistics project presented in this paper.

2. The Austrian Variety of the German Language

German is the official language in Austria, and it is a pluricentric language, "i.e. a language with several interacting centers, each providing a national variety with at least some of its own (codified) norms" (Clyne, 1995: 20). As a pluricentric language German has three standard varieties (Schmidlin, 2011), i.e. German, Austrian and Swiss. However, studies in the field of language geography have shown that the German standards do not follow national borders but rather dialect boundaries (Elspaß et al, 2017). Therefore, the German language is rather a pluriareal (and not a pluricentric) language, making the collection and proper documentation of language resources for the Austrian variety more challenging.

The Austrian variety of the German language differs from the other varieties of German in several aspects (Wiesinger, 1988; Scheuringer, 2001), including lexical differences, pronunciation, the grammatical gender of nouns, the use of tenses or prepositions or the creation of diminutives or composita (Wiesinger, 1996). However, also within the Austrian standard variety differences between regions can be observed.

Moreover, language varieties in Austria, such as dialects are strongly related to a person's identity. Discussions about these varieties are, therefore, often ideological ones (Scheuringer, 1997; Cillia, 1995).

Within this framework, the citizen linguistics project "On everyone's mind and lips – German in Austria" was launched.

3. The Citizen Linguistics Project "On everyone's mind and lips – German in Austria"

The project "On everyone's mind and lips – German in Austria" (abbreviated as IamDiÖ in German) addresses the use and perception of the German language in Austria as well as the attitude of people towards it.

IamDiÖ consists of three project strands, each of which adopts another approach to citizen science. The first strand is entitled Question of the Month. It is aimed at co-creation which means that citizens can raise, and answer research questions related to the topic of German language in Austria. In defining the topic and question, selecting and applying methods to collect and/or analyze data and in interpreting the results, citizens should be supported by scholars, i.e. experts in the field of linguistics.

The second project strand addresses linguistic landscapes, which are defined as "the visibility and salience of languages on public and commercial signs in a given territory or region" (Landry and Bourhis, 1997, 23). Linguistic landscapes thus comprise street names, shop signs, billboard advertisements and stickers on lampposts, among others. A linguistic landscape serves different functions and may help to mark the relative status of linguistic communities in a certain region, among others (Landry and Bourhis, 1997). In order to be able to analyze a linguistic landscape, data in the form of pictures of written information in the public sphere, e.g. pictures of posters, shop signs or stickers on bicycle racks are needed.

The third strand of the project is a meme contest, in which citizens generate data in the form of memes. Citizens are asked to combine text written in a dialect with pictures that can be associated with Austria. Since the creation of memes and their distribution via social media is rather an experiment than citizen science, this strand would not be regarded as citizen science, or rather citizen humanities, per se (Eitzel *et al.*, 2017; Heigl *et al.*, 2019).

In the following sections, the two citizen science strands are elaborated in more detail.

3.1 The Question of the Month

Co-creation is defined as public participation in scholarly research that sees citizens as co-researchers who are involved in any step and decision throughout the research process (Bonney *et al.*, 2009). IamDiÖ intended to apply co-creation in the project's Question of the Month strand. This strand can be considered as a proof of concept for the idea of applying co-creation in citizen linguistics.

3.1.1 Co-creation in Citizen Linguistics

The idea behind the Question of the Month is that volunteers are involved and have a say in the entire research process. They are considered co-researchers. As the name of this project strand already suggests, it addresses research questions. These should be raised and, ideally, also be answered by citizens themselves. Researchers (only) support the volunteers in finding an answer to their questions, e.g. by helping select a method, suggest relevant literature or interpret the results. A Question of the Month should cover language use, language perception or language attitude with a focus on the German language in Austria, including all its varieties. Citizens can submit their questions via the IamDiÖ website. However, the number of questions collected during science communication events, such as the Long Night of Research in Austria or the Austrian Science Fund's Science and Society Festival, was tremendously higher, amounting to about 500 questions that were raised by citizens. These included question such as: "Do dialects in Austria disappear?", "Why do I have to face discrimination because I am from Germany and speak German German?" or "Does communication in social networks have a negative influence on 'good' German?". The volunteers who raised the questions were also asked if they would be willing to find an answer to their question. However, almost all of them refused to do research on their own, even if researchers offered their support. Therefore, the initial attempt of co-created research was foiled already in an early stage of the research process. This is also the reason why the co-creation approach could no longer be adopted in the project. Subsequently, the idea of the Question of the Month had to be re-considered as well.

3.1.2 From Co-creation to Science Communication

Instead of asking citizens to answer the research questions, the scholars in the project were required to respond to the questions. After all these questions had been collected from citizens, they were clustered according to topic. Every month, two questions per theme are selected by the project team. Here, the initial idea that two questions are selected, and in social networks citizens vote for the question that should be answered this month could still be put into action. After the users have voted for their favorite question, the question getting most of the votes is answered by the researchers. The scholars give an answer to the research question in a blog entry that follows a uniform structure. This structure reflects the research process and related steps, i.e. finding a topic, defining a research question, doing a literature review, selecting a method, applying the method, analyzing data, writing about the results, interpreting the results and drawing conclusions. In this case, the conclusions are not only related to the research itself but also to the person and the personal development of the academic researcher (or the citizen humanist). This uniform structure that was oriented towards the research process should help readers gain an insight into the steps in the research process and increase academic literacy. As a final step, the scholar's (or citizen humanist's) answer is published as a blog entry on the IamDiÖ website and circulated via social networks. Interestingly, the questions raised by the citizens also helped to reveal research gaps.

Although, the citizens showed interest in the topic and raised a lot of questions in the initial project phase, this interest could not be sustained in the subsequent stages of the research process, thus, shifting the focus from co-creation to science communication in the other project phases.

3.2 Linguistic Landscaping

The second strand of the project can be regarded as collaborative approach to citizen science (Bonney *et al.*, 2009). This IamDiÖ strand is aimed at studying the linguistic landscape in Austria. Participants are asked to collect and analyze data in the form of pictures of written text in the public space, e.g. street names, posters or graffiti containing text. Citizens gather and analyze these pictures with the Lingscape app (Purschke, 2017; Seltmann and Heinisch, 2018).

3.2.1 Linguistic Treasure Hunts

To make linguistic landscape research more appealing to the participants, linguistic treasure hunts are organized in different cities in Austria. Linguistic treasure hunts as a method combine linguistic landscaping done by citizens with gamification. These are treasure hunts modified to the needs of citizen linguistics (with a focus on linguistic landscaping). Similar to treasure hunts in which a group of persons follows clues to get to a certain location, linguistic treasure hunts also have clues that are placed in an urban space and that participants have to solve to get to the next clue to finally win a prize. Since the groups move in the public space when they get from clue to clue, they also walk past written text. This text is interesting for linguistic landscape research, especially for research on language variation in writing. Therefore, with linguistic treasure hunts, scholars can pursue the objective of gathering data on and analyzing (written) language variation in the public sphere. In addition to the tasks completed in a traditional treasure hunt, the groups are tasked with taking, uploading and tagging photographs of written texts in the public sphere. The tagging task plays a crucial role since participants have to add annotations to the pictures, including geographical location, language(s) in which the text is written, language varieties, e.g. dialects, or function, medium and context. In linguistic treasure hunts, data quantity, i.e. the number of pictures uploaded and data quality, i.e. the annotation, have to be balanced: The groups do not only receive points for the number of uploaded photographs but also for the tags (according to a point system). Finally, a prize is given to the group who followed all the clues, uploaded the most pictures and annotated them in accordance with predefined criteria (Heinisch, in print b).

3.2.2 Recruitment through Citizen Science Award

This project strand could recruit some participants through the Austrian Citizen Science Award, which is an event that helps citizen science projects recruit participants, i.e. school classes and individuals. Within a specified period of time, these classes and individuals can contribute to a range of citizen science projects. These contributions can be data collection, data analysis, etc. The most successful classes and persons receive prizes from each citizen science project in a festive ceremony.

For linguistic landscaping, the instructions for the participants were to take pictures of written text in the public space and upload, geolocate and tag them with the *Lingscape* app. The individuals with the highest number of pictures uploaded (and tagged) win the prize, whereas the class with the highest amount of uploaded (and tagged) pictures and who, additionally, submitted a research report receives the prize.

4. Language Resources

The language resources created by these two project strands address the diversity of the Austrian variety of the German language and the diverse use of language(s) in Austria.

First, the language resource comprising the Questions of the Month (IamDiÖ, 2019) is a corpus of questions and answers addressing the Austrian variety of the German language. These questions and answers range from the use of language(s) and their varieties in Austria, language change, perception of and attitudes towards language(s) and their varieties. While this monolingual corpus has a clear thematic focus on the Austrian variety of the German language, the corpus itself is in both Austrian and German standard varieties since the academics (and citizen humanists) writing the answers have diverse language backgrounds. Although this corpus is not annotated, it has a clear structure. As mentioned before, the corpus consists of questions and answers according to a predefined structure derived from the steps in the scholarly research process. This monolingual written corpus in German is available under a Creative Commons licence. It is newly created and constantly added to. This language resource lends itself to information retrieval and extraction, knowledge discovery or representation or machine learning.

Second, the data collected through the linguistic treasure hunts may not be regarded as language resource *sensu stricto*, since the pictures containing text are only available as pictures (IamDiÖ & Lingscape, 2019). Optical character recognition has not been used so far, but the pictures are annotated according to an annotation scheme, which was developed by the IamDiÖ team for the linguistic treasure hunts (Heinisch, in print b). The pictures and annotations made during the linguistic treasure hunts were integrated into the *Lingscape* database, which is a (partially) annotated database of photographs of text written in different languages found in the public sphere. This database is, therefore, a compilation of pictures and annotations from different projects aimed at the analysis of linguistic landscapes in different countries. To make this resource available for further use, e.g. natural language processing, it would need further preparatory work.

5. Comparison of Collaborative and Co-created Project Strands

A comparison of the two project strands focusing on citizen linguistics should reveal the success of each. However, a comparison proved challenging not only because each citizen science project defines success differently (Freitag and Pfeffer, 2013), but also due to the different approaches and topics of these strands. The criteria used for the comparative analysis were the number of participants, the number of contributions (per participant) and perceived advancement in scholarship (Heinisch, in print a). It must be noted that this study was not planned in advance. It was only implemented after the first phase of the project ended. This means that no rigid data collection principles had been defined beforehand, but all the available data (including estimations) were aggregated only afterwards to answer the question of which project strand was more successful.

5.1 Criteria

Despite the ongoing debate on success in the citizen science literature and criteria defined (Cox *et al.*, 2015; Freitag and Pfeffer, 2013), the available data made it necessary to specify own criteria, namely the number of participants, the number of contributions per participant and perceived advancement in scholarship (Table 1). The number of participants had to be partly estimated since no rigid counting of science festival visitors was applied. The (average) contributions per participant are based on the overall number of contributions and the (estimated) number of participants. Contributions to the Question of the Month project strand are the (average) number of research questions raised per participant, whereas contributions to the linguistic treasure hunts are the (average) number of pictures uploaded to the app. The perceived advancement to scholarship is based on the author's personal perception of the contribution of each of the activities to scholarly knowledge or academia in general. Finally, Table 1 also contains information on the degree of voluntariness, which will be elaborated later (Heinisch, in print a).

5.2 Comparison

The comparative analysis (Heinisch, in print a) demonstrated that the project strand aimed at co-creation attracted more participants overall (but only in the initial research phase in which the task was to find a research question) (Table 1). This is in contrast to the number of contributions per participant that were significantly higher for the linguistic treasure hunts. These differences in numbers may be attributed to various factors. The most obvious one is that the topic of German in Austria was appealing to a high number of people and the data, i.e. the research questions for the Question of the Month were collected from visitors of science communication festivals based on personal dialogue. This allowed for the collection of about 500 questions in total. The comparison between the Question of the Month and the linguistic treasure hunt demonstrated that the task of crowdsourcing, i.e. soliciting contributions from the crowd, i.e. a large group of unfamiliar individuals (Bowser and Shanley, 2013), yielded the better results regarding data quantity (Heinisch, in print a).

Another category in which the project strands were compared was the degree of voluntariness, which can be related to a person's motivation for participating in a certain citizen science activity. The practice of involving school classes or university students in citizen science, raises the issue of voluntary participation, since the citizen science tasks are often mandatory parts in a school subject or university course.

According to the Oxford English Dictionary (2020), voluntariness is "[t]he state or condition of being voluntary, free, or unconstrained; absolute freedom or liberty in respect of choice, determination, or action". In addition to openness and collaboration, voluntariness is one of the basic ideas in citizen science (Fresa and Justrell, 2015). Therefore, the study (Heinisch, in print a) differentiated between three degrees of voluntariness, i.e. voluntary (the participants freely decided to participate in the task at hand, e.g. based on their interest in the topic), semi-voluntary (the participants were given an incentive to participate, but the decision to take part in the activity was taken freely) and non-voluntary (which includes some type of compulsion). This categorisation shows a strong link to the debate on intrinsic and extrinsic motivation. It is assumed that especially non-voluntary participation may negatively affect motivation, data quality and data quantity. However, these needs to be further investigated.

When comparing the Question of the Month and the linguistic treasure hunt from the point of view of voluntariness, the Question of the Month boosts a higher degree of voluntariness, since the majority of the questions were raised out of curiosity. As the questions were primarily collected during science communication events, the citizens' contributions can be considered voluntary ones since only people who are interested in the topic enter a project's festival booth. Nevertheless, also the Question of the Month strand had some semi-voluntary contributions, since university students were encouraged to deliver questions and/or answers. Here, for some university students the submission of research questions was a mandatory part of a course. In other university courses it was no compulsory assignment but a semi-voluntary one, since students could get bonus points for a course. In general, only one participant (from the bonus point group) was willing to answer her own research question.

For the linguistic treasure hunts, which were organized several times in Austrian cities throughout the project, semi-voluntary participation prevailed. This is due to the fact that the majority of the participants were university students receiving bonus points.

While we can assume that participation of individuals in the Citizen Science Award is semi-voluntary, and either driven by intrinsic motivation or the prize incentive, the participation of the school classes can be regarded as semi-voluntary (the teachers may participate out of interest in the topic and/or to win a prize for the class; but their class must participate since the citizen science activities are part of the relevant subject at school).

In general, the number of pictures uploaded was higher if there was an incentive, either bonus points for university students or a prize. This increase in data quantity due to the prize incentive especially held true for the individuals who participated in the Citizen Science Award competition.

The contributions to the advancement in scholarship differ significantly between the two project strands. While the linguistic treasure hunts could primarily increase the amount of (partially) annotated data for linguistic landscaping research, the Question of the Month strand revealed knowledge and research gaps, helped raise new questions, challenged established approaches in academia and questioned paradigms (in scholarly research). Since one participant found an answer to her research question without the help of scholars, but according to the principles of academic research, also independent research could be observed.

6. Discussion

There is a growing body of literature that recognizes motivation in citizen science (Moczek, 2019; Oded Nov, Ofer Arazy, David Anderson, 2011; Raddick *et al.*, 2010), but far too little attention has been paid to the voluntariness of participation. Studies of gamification in citizen science show the importance of data quality and motivation (Tinati *et al.*, 2017; Curtis, 2015; Prestopnik and Crowston, 2011). Gamification was also an inherent part of the linguistic treasure hunts. Gamification, which is accompanied by competition, helped to strengthen the motivation of treasure hunt participants and increased the amount of data gathered, but it also may impede data quality, especially the quality of the annotations (Heinisch, in print b). Finding the right balance between data quantity and data quality is also a major area of interest in citizen science (Bordogna *et al.;* Crall *et al.;* Ellwood *et al.*, 2016; Hunter *et al.*, 2013; Kelling *et al.;* Kosmala *et al.*, 2016; Prats López, 2017). Means of quality control and evaluation could also help to increase the quality of the data gathered during linguistic treasure hunts.

7. Conclusion

Language resources are a major ingredient for the advancement of language technologies. Citizen linguistics can help to create language resources and annotate language resources. This is important not only for the improvement of language technologies, such as machine translation but also for the advancement of linguistic research.

Exemplified by the citizen linguistics project "On everyone's mind and lips – German in Austria", two approaches to citizen linguistics were compared, i.e. an attempt to implement co-creation in the citizen humanities (the Question of the Month) on the one hand, and a collaborative approach to linguistic landscaping (including linguistic treasure hunts), on the other. The (language) resources created by these two approaches are a corpus related to the Question of the Month project strand and a partially annotated database of pictures of written text in different languages and language varieties found in the public sphere.

The number of participants in these two project strands differed significantly. Especially those activities that were related to data collection (and analysis) had a significantly higher number of contributions per participant. This especially held true for the activities with (prize) incentives. Nevertheless, the activities of the Question of the Month that aimed at co-creation could reach a higher number of participants, even after the co-creation approach was no longer followed. In addition, especially the Question of the Month brought research gaps and new knowledge to light and challenged existing paradigms and practices.

Citizen linguistics can help gather and analyze linguistic data, including language resources, in a short period of time. Thus, it may help increase the access to and availability of language resources, including language resources particular to a certain language variety, e.g. language resources in standard varieties or dialects. Therefore, citizen linguistics can play a crucial role in the advancement of language technologies and scholarly research.

8. Acknowledgements

This work has been partly funded by the Austrian Science Fund (FWF): TCS 57-G.

Project strand	Communication	Number of participants	Number of contributions per participant	Contribution to advancement in scholarship	Voluntariness/motivation
Question of the Month (QM)	QM Festivals	350 (estimation)	1-5 (estimation)	New research topics Challenging established approaches/paradigms	Voluntary/interest
	QM university courses	20 (two universities)	1	Partly independent research into their individual questions	Incentive: part of the course or bonus points for the course
	QM web form and e-mail	4	4	New research topics Challenging established approaches/paradigms	Voluntary/interest
Linguistic landscaping (LL)	LL treasure hunts	20 (two cities)	16 (on average) (with prize: 29; without prize 7)	Data collection and initial analysis	Voluntary (4 persons) Bonus point for course (16 persons) Incentive: prize vs no prize
	LL Austrian Citizen Science Award	4 registered individuals 7 registered school classes	83 (individual) 38 (school)	Data collection and initial analysis Partly: new research topics	Incentive: prize

Table 1 : Comparison of the two project strands Question of the Month and linguistic landscaping (in July 2019)

9. Bibliographical References

Bonney, R., Ballard, H., Jordan, R., McCallie, E., Phillips, T., Shirk, J. et al. (2009) Public Participation in Scientific Research: Defining the Field and Assessing Its Potential for Informal Science Education. http://files.eric.ed.gov/fulltext/ED519688.pdf (last accessed February 11, 2016).

Bordogna, G., Carrara, P., Criscuolo, L., Pepe, M. and Rampini, A. A linguistic decision making approach to assess the quality of volunteer geographic information for citizen science. Information Sciences, 10 February 2014, Vol.258, pp.312-327, 312.

Bowser, A. and Shanley, L. A. (2013) New Visions in Citizen Science. https://www.wilsoncenter.org/sites/default/files/NewVisionsInCitizenScience.pdf (last accessed August 28, 2017).

Cillia, R. de (1995) Deutsche Sprache und österreichische Identität. Medienimpulse, 4, 4–13.

Cox, J., Oh, E. Y., Simmons, B., Lintott, C., Masters, K., Greenhill, A. et al. (2015) Defining and Measuring Success in Online Citizen Science. A Case Study of Zooniverse Projects. Computing in Science & Engineering, 17, 2015: 10.1109/MCSE.2015.65.

Crall, A. W., Newman, G. J., Stohlgren, T. J., Holfelder, K. A., Graham, J. and Waller, D. M. Assessing citizen science data quality: an invasive species case study. Conservation Letters, 2011, Vol.4(6), pp.433-442, 433.

Curtis, V. (2015) Motivation to Participate in an Online Citizen Science Game. Science Communication, 37, 2015: 10.1177/1075547015609322.

DiWA (2019) Die Rolle des Wenker-Atlasses in der Geschichte der Dialektologie. http://www.diwa.info/Geschichte/RolleDesWenkeratlasses.aspx.

Eitzel, M. V., Cappadonna, J. L., Santos-Lang, C., Duerr, R. E., Virapongse, A., West, S. E. et al. (2017) Citizen Science Terminology Matters. Exploring Key Terms. Citizen Science: Theory and Practice, 2, 2017: 10.5334/cstp.96.

Ellwood, E., Henry Bart, JR, Doosey, M., Jue, D., Mann, J., Nelson, G. et al. (2016) Mapping Life – Quality Assessment of Novice vs. Expert Georeferencers. Citizen Science: Theory and Practice, 1, 2016: 10.5334/cstp.30.

Freitag, A. and Pfeffer, M. J. (2013) Process, not product: investigating recommendations for improving citizen science « success ». PloS one, 8, 2013: 10.1371/journal.pone.0064079.

Fresa, A. and Justrell, B. (2015) Roadmap for Citizen Science. https://www.civic-epistemologies.eu/wp-content/uploads/2014/08/CE_Roadmap-Handbook.pdf.

Heigl, F., Kieslinger, B., Paul, K. T., Uhlik, J. and Dörler, D. (2019) Opinion: Toward an international definition of citizen science. Proceedings of the National Academy of Sciences of the United States of America, 116, 2019: 10.1073/pnas.1903393116.

Heinisch, B. (in print a) Comparison of co-created and collaborative approaches to citizen science adopted by the citizen linguistics project 'On everyone's mind and lips – German in Austria'. In, Proceedings of the 5th Austrian Citizen Science Conference 2019, 26-28, June, 2019, Obergurgl, Austria.

Heinisch, B. (in print b) Hunting for signs in the public space – the method of linguistic treasure hunts as a form of citizen science. In, Proceedings of the 5th Austrian Citizen Science Conference 2019, 26-28, June, 2019, Obergurgl, Austria.

Herrgen, J. (2010) The digital wenker atlas (www.diwa.info): an online research tool for modern dialectology. Dialectología, 95.

Hunter, J., Alabri, A. and Ingen, C. (2013) Assessing the quality and trustworthiness of citizen science data. Concurrency and Computation: Practice and Experience, 25, 454–66.

Kelling, S., Fink, D., Sorte, F., Johnston, A., Bruns, N. and Hochachka, W. Taking a 'Big Data' approach to data quality in a citizen science project. Ambio, 2015, Vol.44(4), pp.601-611, 601.

Kosmala, M., Wiggins, A., Swanson, A. and Simmons, B. (2016) Assessing data quality in citizen science. Frontiers in Ecology and the Environment, 14, 2016: 10.1002/fee.1436.

Landry, R. and Bourhis, R. Y. (1997) Linguistic Landscape and Ethnolinguistic Vitality. Journal of Language and Social Psychology, 16, 1997: 10.1177/0261927X970161002.

Moczek, N. (2019) Freiwilliges Engagement für Citizen Science-Projekte im Naturschutz: Konstruktion und Validierung eines Skalensystems zur Messung motivationaler und organisationaler Funktionen, 1. Auflage. Lengerich, Pabst Science Publishers.

ÖAW-ACDH Wörterbuch der bairischen Mundarten in Österreich (WBÖ). https://vawadioe.acdh.oeaw.ac.at/projekte/wboe/wboe-startseite/.

Oded Nov, Ofer Arazy, David Anderson (2011) Technology-Mediated Citizen Science Participation: A Motivational Model. In, Proceedings of the Fifth International AAAI Conference on Weblogs and Social Media.

Oxford English Dictionary (OED) (2020)Voluntariness, Oxford University Press.

Prats López, M. (2017) Managing Citizen Science in the Humanities: The challenge of ensuring quality, Vrije Universiteit. http://hdl.handle.net/1871/55271.

Prestopnik, N. R. and Crowston, K. (2011) Gaming for (Citizen) Science: Exploring Motivation and Data Quality in the Context of Crowdsourced Science through the Design and Evaluation of a Social-Computational System. In, 2011 IEEE Seventh International Conference on e-Science Workshops. IEEE, pp. 28–33.

Purschke, C. (2017) Crowdsourcing the linguistic landscape of a multilingual country. Introducing Lingscape in Luxembourg, 2017: 10.13092/lo.85.4086.

Raddick, M. J., Bracey, G., Gay, P. L., Lintott, C. J., Murray, P., Schawinski, K. et al. (2010) Galaxy Zoo. Exploring the Motivations of Citizen Science Volunteers. Astronomy Education Review, 9, 2010: 10.3847/AER2009036.

Scheuringer, H. (1997) Sprachvarietäten in Österreich. In Stickel, G. (ed), Varietäten des Deutschen: Regional- und Umgangssprachen. Berlin, New York, de Gruyter, pp. 332–345.

Seltmann, M. E.-H. and Heinisch, B. (2018) How to speak German in Austria. Collaboration between two linguistic citizen science projects – "On everyone's

mind and lips – German in Austria" and "Lingscape" found each other, FRONTIERS MEDIA SA. https://klf.univie.ac.at/fileadmin/user_upload/p_klf/Proceedings_OECSK2018.pdf, 82–85.
Stöckle, P. (2019) Wie ein Dialektwörterbuch entsteht. https://dioe.at/details/artikel/1963/.
Tinati, R., Luczak-Roesch, M., Simperl, E. and Hall, W. (2017) An investigation of player motivations in Eyewire, a gamified citizen science project. Computers in Human Behavior, 73, 2017: 10.1016/j.chb.2016.12.074.
WBÖ (2020) Materialbasis. https://vawadioe.acdh.oeaw.ac.at/projekte/wboe/materialbasis/.

10. Language Resource References

IamDiÖ. (2019). Frage des Monats, https://iam.dioe.at/frage-des-monats/beantwortete-fragen/
IamDiÖ & Lingscape (2019). Lingscape https://lingscape.carto.com/builder/781d0814-ef0d-11e6-ad6f-0e3ff518bd15/

Proceedings of the LREC 2020 Workshop "Citizen Linguistics in Language Resource Development", pages 15–25
Language Resources and Evaluation Conference (LREC 2020), Marseille, 11–16 May 2020

Objective Assessment of Subjective Tasks in Crowdsourcing Applications

Giannis Haralabopoulos, Myron Tsikandilakis, Mercedes Torres Torres, Derek McAuley
University of Nottingham
name.surname@nottingham.ac.uk

Abstract

Labelling, or annotation, is the process by which we assign labels to an item with regards to a task. In some Artificial Intelligence problems, such as Computer Vision tasks, the goal is to obtain objective labels. However, in problems such as text and sentiment analysis, subjective labelling is often required. More so when the sentiment analysis deals with actual emotions instead of polarity (positive/negative) . Scientists employ human experts to create these labels, but it is costly and time consuming. Crowdsourcing enables researchers to utilise non-expert knowledge for scientific tasks. From image analysis to semantic annotation, interested researchers can gather a large sample of answers via crowdsourcing platforms in a timely manner. However, non-expert contributions often need to be thoroughly assessed, particularly so when a task is subjective. Researchers have traditionally used 'Gold Standard', 'Thresholding' and 'Majority Voting' as methods to filter non-expert contributions. We argue that these methods are unsuitable for subjective tasks, such as lexicon acquisition and sentiment analysis. We discuss subjectivity in human centered tasks and present a filtering method that defines quality contributors, based on a set of objectively infused terms in a lexicon acquisition task. We evaluate our method against an established lexicon, the diversity of emotions - i.e. subjectivity- and the exclusion of contributions. Our proposed objective evaluation method can be used to assess contributors in subjective tasks that will provide domain agnostic, quality results, with at least 7% improvement over traditional methods.
Keywords: Natural Language Processing, Crowdsourcing, Lexicon, Subjectivity, Objectivity

1. Introduction

Data is the most sought-after commodity of the digital era. Through interaction, expression and reasoning we produce varying types of data. From a philosophical standpoint, there are two main categories of information embedded in data: objective and subjective information. Objective information relates to empirical facts and their measurement, while subjective information relates to the personal experience and expression of thoughts, opinions and emotions. In the digital space, the objectivity and subjectivity of the information can be linked to human factors. As humans interact with the digital world, the information they share is subject to analysis from scientists and commercial stakeholders. The most common analysis performed, in human submitted digital information, is sentiment analysis (Yue et al., 2018).

Sentiment analysis aims to explore the subjective emotions conveyed in information (Chaturvedi et al., 2018; Yoshino et al., 2018), such as multimedia or simple text sources (Miao et al., 2018; Öztürk and Ayvaz, 2018). With regard to textual information, crowdsourcing is most frequently used to obtain the emotion conveyed in paragraphs of text (Li et al., 2018). Their analysis requires the emotional labelling of full sentences, part of sentences, or terms (Hazarika et al., 2018).

If labelling within the corpus is extensive, then supervised sentiment analysis methods can be applied (Zhao et al., 2018). On the other hand, if no labelling is available, unsupervised methods will need to be employed (Fernández-Gavilanes et al., 2018). If the labelling required to annotate the corpus is extensive, then an unsupervised approach might be a better method (Fernández-Gavilanes et al., 2018). However supervised learning generally obtains better results in most machine learning problems (Schouten et al., 2018).

Expert labelling is both expensive and time consuming (Palan and Schitter, 2018). As an alternative, crowdsourcing enables scientists to recruit a higher number of individuals to improve the quality of the labelling process through redundancy. Crowdsourcing is the process of non-expert annotators contributing to scientific tasks (Howe, 2006). Crowdsourcing platforms provide access to a diverse range of contributors (Peer et al., 2017). Data gathered for sentiment analysis favors distinct classes rather than a distribution of classes (Koltsova et al., 2016; O'Leary, 2016). Even when the requested data spans through several categories, the results are filtered based on a gold standard (Tang et al., 2015; Maynard and Bontcheva, 2016).

Polarity, i.e. positive and negative emotion, is a common topic of interest that leads to refined polarity and extended to pure emotion or beyond polarity analysis (Basile et al., 2018; Sharma and Chakraverty, 2018). In polarity-based annotation tasks, contributors are tasked with deciding between a positive or a negative label (Budhi et al., 2018), Conversely, in a refined or pure emotion analysis annotators are labeling text using either a scale from negative to positive, or the provided emotional list respectively (Ghosal et al., 2018).

The gold standard is used to filter spam or dishonest responses. It is based on predefined expected answers. It is widely used in image analysis and crowdsourcing applications (Ghosh et al., 2015). It has also been used in the subjective evaluation of emotional information (Calefato et al., 2017), alongside with majority voting (Zamil et al., 2019), to determine the most appropriate label for a term, group or sentence. Majority voting methods appoint the most annotated emotion as the corresponding emotion label. Information loss occurs in both methods since the annotations that are not part of the major/gold class are excluded. Additionally, these methods fail to address the subjective nature of emotion labelling.

We argue that the aforementioned dominant class selection

methods disregard human subjectivity. In a subjective labelling task, single class or ground truth do not accurately portray the diversity of human evaluation. We propose the use of emotion vectors to retain subjectivity, and the evaluation of contributions based on infused objectively emotional terms. We perform a set of subjective crowdsourcing tasks to assess our proposed method, in which we evaluate participants through their performance solely on terms of objective emotional significance.

The main contributions of this paper are: a contributor evaluation method for subjective crowdsourcing tasks and the use of objective terms based on the subjective task itself. We also highlight the differences of our quality assessed resource when compared to an established pure emotion lexicon.

2. Subjectivity

Subjectivity has been defined as "[...] the lived diversity in experience due to the physical, political and cultural context of [an] experience" (Ellis and Flaherty, 1992). This definition could be a rally point for enabling us to understand the concept of emotion as a universal experience with subjective variability.

For example, there are widely accepted concepts of "universals" in research relating to emotion. These include the theory of universal emotions proposed by Ekman and Friesen (Ekman and Friesen, 1971) and the theory of primary bipolar emotions as suggested by Plutchik (Plutchik, 1980). According to these seminal social and psychological theories anger, fear, happiness (or joy), disgust, sadness and surprise, and also trust and anticipation are emotions that can be encountered cross-culturally (Ekman and Keltner, 1997). These emotions are also suggested to have shared evolutionary neural and physiological functions. These functions involve automatic and involuntary responses to danger (fear) and sudden environmental changes (surprise), social communication of positive (happiness, joy, trust) and negative states (anger, sadness) and responses to potentially harmful pathogens and nourishment (disgust) (Pessoa and Adolphs, 2010). In a sense these emotions are a "universal language".

The aforementioned definition of subjectivity included the phrase "cultural diversity". Cultural diversity is one of the most widely studied correlates of subjectivity for emotional annotation (Elfenbein, 2017). Contemporary research has found that although there are basic and/or primary emotions that could, indeed, be a "universal language", there are also culture-specific "dialects". These dialects are used for displaying these emotions in terms of facial expressions (Elfenbein and Ambady, 2002). They are also used for communicating culturally-appropriate emotional intensity in written and verbal expressions (Elfenbein and Luckman, 2016). These cultural dialects are suggested to confer an own-culture emotional recognition advantage in response to own-culture stimuli. They are also, arguably, suggested to confer an other-culture emotional recognition bias in response to other-culture stimuli that are distinctly different to the culture of the respondent (Keith, 2019). This is suggested to occur due to the non-convergent social evolution that takes place in different geographical areas. This could mean that although we all understand basic emotions such as fear and happiness, we may display (show) and decode (understand) these emotions differently due to our cultural background (Elfenbein, 2017).

For example, previous research has shown that Western individuals use high-intensity emotional words during social interactions (Semnani-Azad and Adair, 2013). It has also been suggested that Western individuals are not likely to recognise low-intensity expressions of emotion; possibly because these are not accurately discriminated as communicating salient emotional information (Knapp et al., 2013). Conversely, previous research has shown that Eastern individuals use context-specific positive emotional expressions in their social interactions (Masuda et al., 2008). It has also been suggested that Eastern individuals are not likely to acknowledge that a negative in valence expression was part of a social interaction. This is suggested to occur because the acknowledgement would necessitate a negative and culturally inappropriate social response (Matsumoto et al., 2013).

In the same manner, the valence and the meaning we attribute to words and images can be different between cultures (Lauka et al., 2018), between genders (Chaplin, 2015) and between age groups (Silvers et al., 2016). For example, the word "fight", as well as images that show virtual violence (Yao et al., 2017), are often considered to convey positive high arousal in young male respondents. The same stimuli have been shown to elicit neutral and negative emotional responses in older adults, irrespective of gender, and female participants; irrespective of age (Gohier et al., 2013; Reidy et al., 2016). Similar effects, such as differential positive or negative or neutral responses to high-arousal words, have also been reported due to differences in political orientation, religious affiliation and emotional sensitivity (Smith, 2015).

Subjectivity can also occur in response to seemingly innocuous stimuli due to differences in physical experiences such as bodily needs and even illness (Teo, 2018). For example, the on-screen presentation of the, arguably, neutral words "dinner" and "food" has been shown to elicit idiosyncratic annotating, behavioural, physiological and neural responses in specific populations. Individuals who are suffering from an eating disorder (Canetti et al., 2002) and also healthy individuals who have been subjected to mild food deprivation and transient insulin-induced hypoglycemia (Brody et al., 2004) have been shown to label the words "dinner" and "food" as high emotional intensity items.

Accordingly, subjectivity is an important, multi-sided and possibly unavoidable aspect of human interactions. The challenge at hand is how to best incorporate subjectivity in our coding-response framework without treating it as participant error or response bias while at the same time controlling for participant error and response bias (Rouder et al., 2016).

3. Sentiment Analysis

Sentiment analysis is, in its core, a subjective process (Mihalcea et al., 2007). As mentioned above, sentiment analysis can be performed with or without manual labelling; such as supervised or unsupervised methods. Supervised sentiment analysis and other similar methods that utilise a lexicon require a level of manual input. That manual input can be obtained by the scientists themselves, or via crowdsourcing. Crowdsourcing has been used as a method to obtain a large number of manual inputs from an equally large number of contributors. Multiple contributors can be used to obtain an emotion per word association (Kiritchenko and Mohammad, 2017), and a ranked order of words on a best to worst emotional scale. Crowd contributors can identify events, perform predictions and provide emotional annotations for the available data (Schumaker et al., 2016). Subjective topics, such as the discussion and promotion of creative ideas, can also be analysed via the crowd (O'Leary, 2016).

Often, the crowdsourcing inputs need to be evaluated, particularly when the task is objective. The gold standard method described in the introduction is one form of manual evaluation. The evaluation is usually performed by individuals with certain expertise in the task. The definition of experts is most commonly vague and their appointment is often biased. For example, previous publications have provided such definitions of expertise as "three experts in the smartphone industry" (Chamlertwat et al., 2012), "the two authors plus one other colleague" (Diakopoulos and Shamma, 2010), "10 financial experts" (Ranco et al., 2015), "post-graduate students who have at least three years' experience for the respective product domains" (Lau et al., 2014), or did not include further elaboration in regard to the description of the included experts (Kang and Park, 2014; Prabowo and Thelwall, 2009; Hutto and Gilbert, 2014; Caselli et al., 2016).

Expert evaluation of subjective tasks should be reconsidered (Eickhoff, 2018). The relevance (Luhrmann, 2006) and role (Kittur et al., 2008) of expert assessment in subjective topics, such as sentiment analysis, is debated (for a comprehensive review, see Hetmanck's review (Hetmank, 2013)). The exact relationship between the experts and the authors, and the prevalent implicit bias of collaborative relations often remain undisclosed. In the case that the experts are not affiliated with the authors but are externally hired (Haralabopoulos et al., 2018; Haralabopoulos and Simperl, 2017) implicit bias could occur due to the monetary reward involved.

4. Proposed methodology

We propose the evaluation of crowd contributors on a set of objective terms. The objective terms can be the emotions themselves or they can stem from the emotion itself, e.g. "joyous" from "joy", "angry" from "anger". A random number of terms is injected into a simple emotion annotation task hosted in Amazon Mechanical Turk[1]. The objective terms appear randomly during the task, are always followed by a subjective term and rotate over emotions, Table 1.

[1] https://www.mturk.com/

Emotion	Objectively Emotional Terms
anticipation	anticipate anticipating anticipated
joy	joyful joyous joy
trust	trusted trustees trusting
fear	feared fears fearful
sad	sad sadly saddened
disgust	disgusted disgusting disgustful
anger	angered angering angerful
surprise	surprised surprising surprisingly

Table 1: Objective Terms

To identify the optimal number of injected terms, we perform four distinct tasks with varying levels of objective terms injected. We ask contributors "What emotion better describes the current word?". The allowed answers are the eight basic emotions, as defined by Plutchik (Plutchik, 1980). We refrained from including a neutral emotional state because it has been shown that there is a low neutrality consensus for text (Valdivia et al., 2018). We assess each contributor with three different methods, majority voting, threshold, and one objective evaluation process.
Let W be a worker with $\{a_1, a_2, ..., a_j\}$ annotations $a \in \{1, 2, ..., k\}$ and $k \in \mathbb{Z}$, towards a set of terms $T = \{t_1, t_2, ..., t_j\}$. Each method is formulated as follows:

4.1. Majority Voting

For each term t the majority class t_m is defined by:

$$t_m = r_t \text{ with } r \in \{1, 2, ..., k\} \tag{1}$$

$$P_t(r_t) \geq P_t(a_n) \forall\, a_n \in \{a_1, a_2, ..., a_j\} \;\&\; a_n \neq r_t, \tag{2}$$

where $P_t(x)$ is the probability of class x appearing in the annotations of term t.
Majority voting discards answers and contributors that were not in agreement with the majority of annotations. Each worker is assessed based on the majority classes that were in line with the supplied annotations; e.g. a task requester can discard annotations from users that disagreed with the majority classes at a given percentage. Most frequently, the majority class is also defined as the "correct" class for each term.

4.2. Threshold

Let $h \in [0, 1]$ be a predefined threshold. A worker W has their annotations discarded if in:

$$\{a_1, a_2, ..., a_j\} \exists\, a_n \mid P(a_n) \geq h \tag{3}$$

Threshold filtering forces diversity, as requesters can discard contributors with a fixed percentage of annotations in a single answer.

4.3. Objective Annotator Evaluation

To apply an objective evaluation of annotators, we inject $\{t'_1, t'_2, ...\}$ terms, into T, that confine the emotional stimuli (Brosch et al., 2010). The classes l' of t' are predetermined, $\in 1, 2, ...k$, and we judge annotator performance via a micro-averaged F1 method:

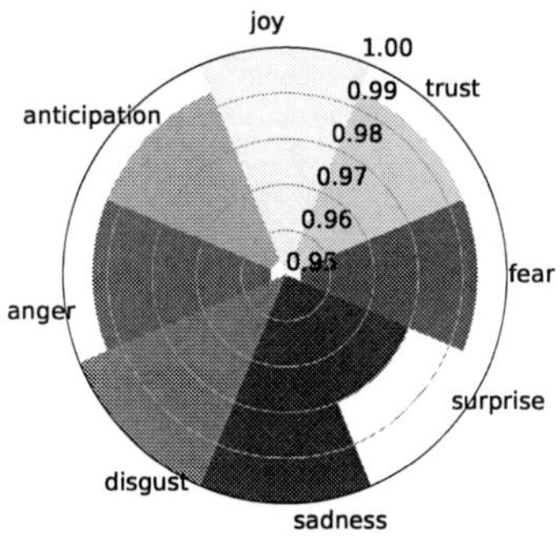

Figure 1: 25%

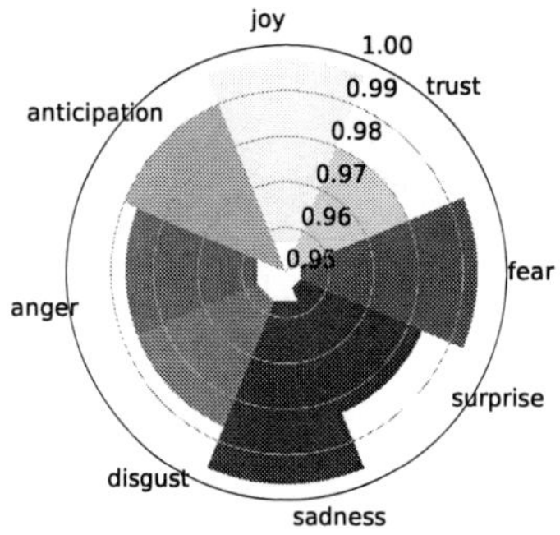

Figure 2: 33%

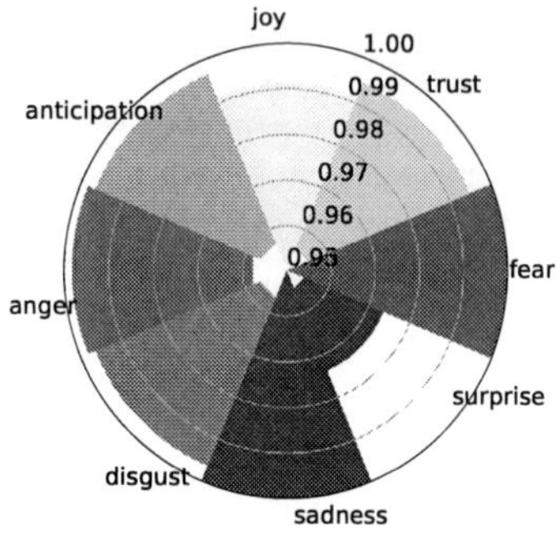

Figure 3: 50%

F1 scores for different objective term injection ratio

		Class l'	$\neq l'$
Annotated	$a' = l'$	*TP*	*FP*
	$a' \neq l'$	*FN*	*TN*

4.3.1. F1 Score

$$precision = \frac{TP}{TP + FP} \tag{4}$$

$$recall = \frac{TP}{TP + FN} \tag{5}$$

$$F1 = \frac{2 * precision * recall}{precision + recall} \tag{6}$$

The algorithmic process can be seen in Algorithm 1. We have a crowdsourcing task, performed by a number of participants. The evaluation method, can be one of the three mentioned above, aims to identify honest contributors. Each participant is evaluated and if deemed honest, is added to the set of quality contributors. Their answers are then returned to the requesters. I.e. the objective terms inside the task function as an honesty assessment.

Algorithm 1: Selection Process Pseudo-Algorithm

Task() = Crowdsourcing Task;
Eval() = Evaluation method;
QC = Set of Quality Contributors;
for *participant* ***in*** *Task()* **do**
    Eval(participant);
    if *Eval(participant)* ***is*** *True* **then**
        add participant **to** QC;
    end
end
return *Task(QC)*

5. Experiment

We inject a set of objective terms, Table 1, into a subjective dataset. The simplicity in task evaluation yields better results (Finnerty et al., 2013) and provides task consistency. Contrary to usual gold standard methods where generic questions are asked to assess the attention of contributors (Aker et al., 2012). The design of the task is based on left to right saccadic movements, consistent with the natural reading patterns of participants as reported in previous research (Starr and Rayner, 2001; White et al., 2015; Smith and Elias, 2018). Although we manually created the objective terms group and regardless of the domain or the task, we can easily obtain a set of objective terms based on the stems and suffixes of the answers.

We choose the subset of common terms found in emotion lexicons, NRC(Mohammad et al., 2013) and PEL (Haralabopoulos et al., 2018; Haralabopoulos and Simperl, 2017). Both lexicons are multi emotion labelled and enable us to select terms with the highest emotional variation, i.e. words with the most diverse emotions annotation.

We created four sub-datasets, based on the ratio of objective to subjective terms. One had no objective terms injected (0%), one had a quarter of subjective terms injected (25%), one had one objective term per two subjective terms (33%) and the final set had the same number of subjective and objective terms (50%). Each term received 10 annotations from 10 different contributors and maximum time per question was 120 seconds.

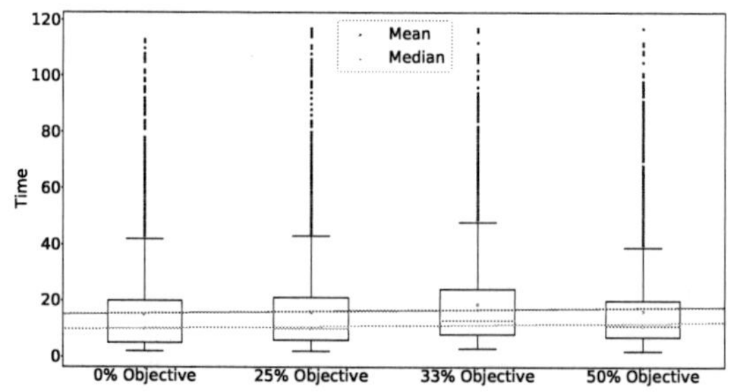

Figure 5: Time Required for Subjective Answers

We present an analysis of the annotators' performance followed by an evaluation section for the results. The evaluation is divided in three parts: a direct correlation analysis of the obtained results and NRC emotion vectors, an emotional diversity analysis and finally a redundacy and exclusion analysis.

5.1. Contributors

The time required, per contributor, to answer each question was analogous to the ratio of injected terms, Figure 5. As the contributors encountered more objective terms, their mean answer time requirement - from 0% to 50% objective terms - went from 14.97s to 16.13s and the median response time from 10s to 11s. An increase of 10% across both metrics indicates an increase of contributors' attention to the task.

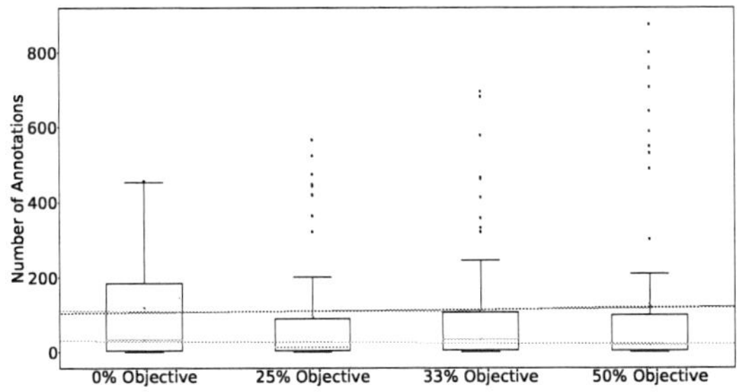

Figure 6: Number of Annotations per Contributor

Tasks occupied an analogous - to the injected terms - number of participants. The 0% task had 39 participants, 25% had 61, while 63 and 73 people contributed to 33% and 50% tasks respectively. Attention requirements of the task negatively affected participation. The task design and layout was consistent throughout all of the tasks, therefore no varying complexity or difficulty factor existed. Due to the increasing number of participants, as the number of injected term increased, the median number of contributions per participant decreased. The mean number of contributions is affected by a large number of major outliers, Figure 6.
With regard to the distribution of objective and subjective terms contributions per participant, the results follow the corresponding injection ratios, slightly affected by contributors with less than 20 subjective answers. Each contributor encountered a median of 20%, 30% and 50% objective terms for their respective injection ratios, Figure 7. The y-axis is the ratio of objective terms to total terms, as encountered by each participant.

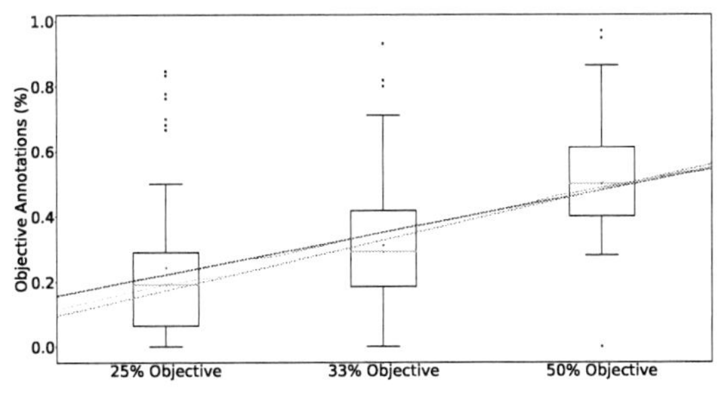

Figure 7: Percent of Objective Annotations per Contributor

The performance of contributors, as measured by our F1 score, was fairly consistent. On average the contributors managed to correctly annotate >96% of the objective terms across all emotions, Figures 1, 2 and 3. The F1 score for surprise-related objective annotations (Table 1) was low in all three different injection ratios. The objective terms for 'sadness', 'fear', and 'joy' had >99% F1. A small variation was observed on the annotation of objective trust terms, especially in the 33% ratio. The number of objective terms does not seem to affect the F1 scores monotonically, since the F1 scores for the objective terms of 33% were worse than those for 50% and 25%. The excluded participants based on a required perfect F1 score where 14 on the highest 50% objective ratio, 11 at 33% and 3 at the 25%.

Injection Ratio	Correct annotations(%)
50	0.9939%
33	0.9892%
25	0.9942%

Table 2: Correct annotation of objective terms for different injection ratios

The distribution of emotions was similar, irrespective of the injection ratio, Figure 12. However, when annotators encountered no objective terms in their task mostly annotated subjective terms as related to trust, joy and disgust. The highest injection ratio (50%) had lower trust and disgust annotation which were redistributed to anger, anticipation and fear. The ratio of objective terms didn't seem to affect the performance of contributors. The overall objective classification accuracy remained around and above 99%, Table 2.

5.2. NRC Correlation

We compare our results to the NRC lexicon (Mohammad et al., 2013). The Spearman's Rho correlation is calculated for each term vector in our results, against the same term vector in NRC. For example, the term '*absolution*' had the following emotional vector in one of our tasks: *[0.0, 0.2, 0.6, 0.0, 0.0, 0.1, 0.1, 0.0]*, and the following vector: *[0.0, 0.5, 0.5, 0.0, 0.0, 0.0, 0.0, 0.0]* in NRC, a correlation of 0.8109. We present Interquartile Range plots for all 456 term correlations in our results and a summarising table with mean and median per term correlation.

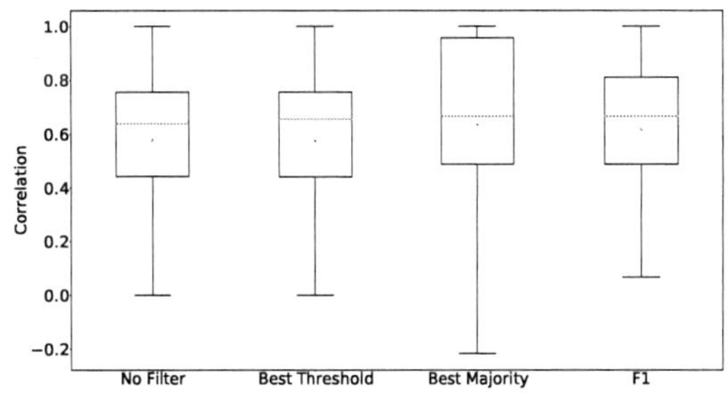

Figure 8: I.Q.R. of per term correlation for all filtering methods, 50% objective terms

For each task of the four crowdsourcing tasks of different injection ratios, we compare the performance of four differ-

Method	a		b	
	Mean	Median	Mean	Median
No filter	0.5781	0.6381	0.5781	0.6381
20% Threshold	0.5578	0.6547	0.5578	0.6547
100% Majority	**0.6498**	0.6547	0.0656	0.0660
F1	0.6191	**0.6667**	**0.6191**	**0.6667**

Table 3: Comparing Spearman's Rho (a) and Adjusted Score (b) for 50% injection ratio

ent filtering methods. No filter method refers to the results as received from the crowdsourcing task. The X% threshold entails the removal of all annotators that annotated more than X% of their terms with the same emotion. To determine the best threshold method for each injection ratio, we calculate the correlation for four different thresholds 20% - 30% - 40% - 50%. For each term, after the end of the task, we determine one or more major emotions. By comparing the annotations of each contributor in relation to the major class(es) of each term we acquire a per contributor majority agreement factor. To obtain the best majority method we calculate the correlation for 100% - 90% - 80% -70% per contributor majority agreement factor. Finally, the F1 method excludes contributors with lower then 100% objective term classification F1 scores. Each method results to a unique lexicon with varying emotional vectors for each term.

On applying the best majority filtering method to the 50% injection ratio, we noticed a remarkably high correlation. Due to the extensive filtering of the results, some methods are evaluated on a small subset of the total 456 terms. Figure 8 presents the IQR of per term correlation values between NRC and the results of the 50% objective ratio task. However, the high correlation of 'Majority' filtering is misleading. The number of terms - post filtering - was 46, which is almost a tenth of the original 456 terms. To better portray lexicon coverage, we assign an *Adjusted Score* to each term as follows:

$$AS = Spearman's\ Rho * \frac{Filtered\ terms}{Total\ terms} \quad (7)$$

'Filtered terms' refers to the number of terms remaining after filtering, while *'Total terms'* is the number of terms used in each task -in our experiments: $Totalterms = 456$. The correlation and the low coverage of Majority filtering is outlined in Table 3 column b in comparison to column a, $(a)\ 0.6498 * \frac{46}{456} = (b)\ 0.0656$.

Adjusted Score (AS) was consistently higher than 0.55 for every task and filtering method. The injection of objective terms improved the AS across all filtering methods, Table 4. In every task the F1 filtering presented the highest low whisker, $Q1 + 1.5 * IQR$. The upper quartile, Q3, was highest for best majority for every task. The majority that yielded the highest correlation with NRC was 70% for 50-33-25 injection ratios, Figure 9(a), 9(b) and 9(c), and 60% for the task with no injection, Figure 9(d). The best threshold was 30% for 50-33-0 injection ratios and 20% for the 25 injection ratio.

Correlation differences per task is relatively low. For 50% injection ratio F1 and Best Majority presents the highest median correlation. Best majority retains a high median correlation for 33% injection ratio, equal to Best Threshold. For the 25% and 0% ratios Best Majority presents the highest correlation. The variance is low for all methods, ranging from $9 * 10^{-5}$ to $4 * 10^{-4}$.

5.3. Emotional Diversity

The emotional diversity is defined as the multitude of annotated emotions per term. The set of Figures 10 presents the regression lines - with 95% confidence interval - of emotional diversity for each filtering method per injection ratio. The x-axis shows the number of different emotions in one term as per NRC, while the y-axis shows the number of different emotions in the same term post filtering.

The F1 filtering consistently provided a high number (> 2) of emotional diversity, Figures 10(a), 10(b) and 10(c). As the injection ratio is reduced the emotional diversity of F1 increased to up to 3 emotions per term.

Threshold filtering was strictly bound to the best performance threshold. When the 30% threshold was used, Figures 10(a),10(b) and 10(d), the number of emotions per term was higher than F1 filtering. However, when the best threshold was 20%, Figure 10(c), the emotions per term falls < 2. On the contrary, when the majority was stricter at 70%, the number of emotions per term was very low, Figures 10(a), 10(b) and 10(c). When the majority was set a lower 60% the emotional diversity increased.

Both threshold and majority filtering methods bound the distributions to their upper limits and directly affect the emotional distribution. Majority filtering was limiting diversity as it required single annotation agreement, while threshold filtering enforced diversity due to limiting peak class annotation.Our proposed F1 filtering is distribution agnostic, thus it doesn't directly alters the emotional diversity of each term.

5.4. Redundancy

Each filtering method had different redundancy and exclusion factors, Figures 11. F1 filtering maintained a redundancy higher than 6 for all injection ratios. As the injection ratio was decreasing, the redundancy level improved. A similar trend was noticed in the emotional diversity analysis, where lower injection ratios resulted in a higher number of emotion annotations. Conversely, Threshold filtering had an analogous to the injection ratio redundancy, probably because it was affected by the tight 20% threshold of the 25% injection ratio, Figure 11(a). Majority filtering had a redundancy lower than 5 throughout all the injection ratios. As the Majority filter lowers to 60%, for the 0% objective terms task, redundancy increases to ≈ 6.

Nonetheless, the exclusion of annotations after filtering was significant, especially for Majority. High Majority requirements result in high exclusion. For all injection ratio the exclusion of annotations was higher than 60%, Figure 11(b). Strict threshold filtering increased exclusion, 25% injection ratio. F1 filtering exclusion was steadily lower than 40%.

6. Conclusions

Honest and non-spam contributions are of major importance for subjective tasks (Haralabopoulos et al., 2019;

Method	50%		33%		25%		0%	
	Mean	Median	Mean	Median	Mean	Median	Mean	Median
No filter	0.5781	**0.6381**	**0.5847**	0.6325	0.561	0.6193	0.5664	0.6193
Best Threshold	0.5777	0.656	**0.6167**	**0.6667**	0.588	0.6503	0.5585	0.6325
Best Majority	0.6379	0.6667	0.6268	0.6667	**0.6415**	**0.6865**	0.6117	0.6614
F1	**0.6191**	**0.6667**	0.5678	0.6325	0.5786	0.6325	*N/A*	*N/A*

Table 4: Mean and Median *Adjusted Score* correlation for different injection ratios

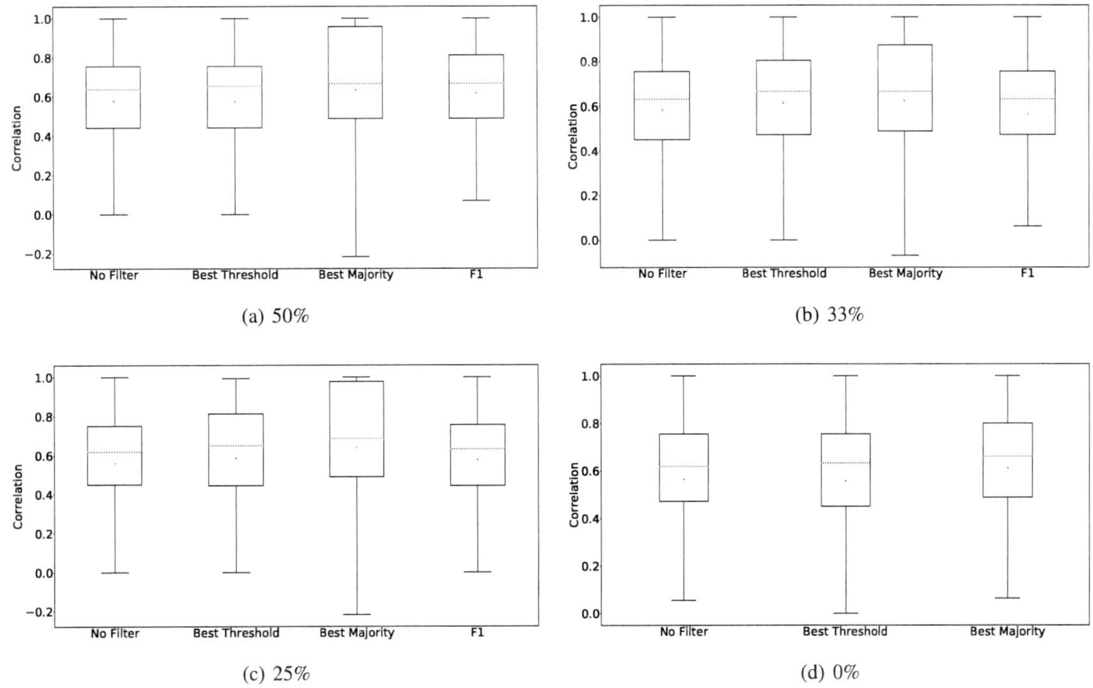

(a) 50% (b) 33%

(c) 25% (d) 0%

Figure 9: I.Q.R. of per term *Adjusted Score* for different objective term inclusion ratios

Jonell et al., 2018). We proposed an evaluation method based on objective terms and the evaluation of contributors based on a F1 contributor score, which is calculated only against the objective terms. The inclusion of objective terms and the filtering of dishonest or spamming annotations in a crowdsourcing task involves a direct resource cost. Requesters will need to allocated extra resources, to inject objective terms in addition to the desired subjective terms, to implement our proposed method. A varying level of injected terms is used to identify the trade-offs and costs of this filtering method.

We evaluated our proposed injection and the F1 filtering method with: correlation co-efficient analysis against an established lexicon, the analysis of the emotional diversity of the resulting terms, term redundancy and annotation exclusion ratio post filtering. Furthermore, we implemented two widely used filtering methods in crowdsourcing, Threshold and Majority, and calculated, based on their NRC correlation, the best performing filter bounds. The best Threshold and Majority filters, for each injection ratio, were also compared to our F1 filter.

Although we used NRC as the baseline for our evaluation, there were major emotional differences amongst the NRC lexicon and our annotation results, Figure 12. The NRC emotions of 'joy', 'fear', 'sadness' and 'anger' are outside the mean standard error range of our task results. Amongst those four emotions, 'joy' is marginalised in NRC when compared to our obtained emotional distributions. On the other hand, the intra-task correlation (0-25-33-50) is relatively high for all emotions. As we used a small subset (456 terms) from NRC, we cannot safely conclude whether the observed effects, of 'joy' suppression and emotional distribution difference, are lexicon-wide.

The inclusion of objective terms in the task improved the per term correlation irrespective of the filtering method. Our proposed F1 filtering method revealed a high correlation co-efficient with NRC, high emotional diversity, high redundancy and low exclusion ratio. F1 filtering improved all metrics when compared to the unfiltered results. Majority voting yielded the highest correlation results with low emotional diversity, low redundancy and high exclusion ratio. Finally, Threshold filtering had high correlation but was limited to the best performing threshold level on all three evaluations of diversity, redundancy and exclusion.

Most importantly, the contributor filtering of our approach doesn't directly affect the distribution of answers. A sub-

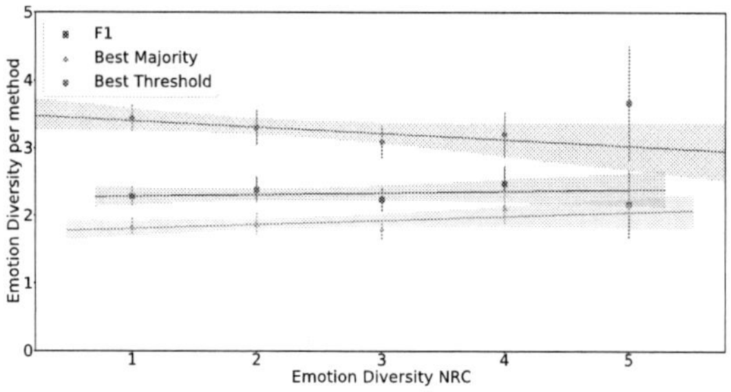

(a) 50%

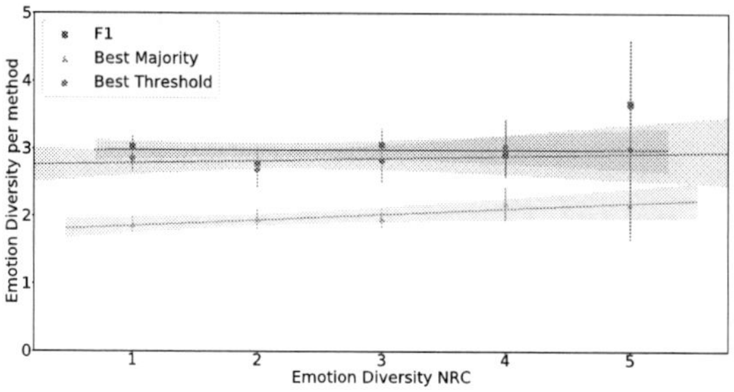

(b) 33%

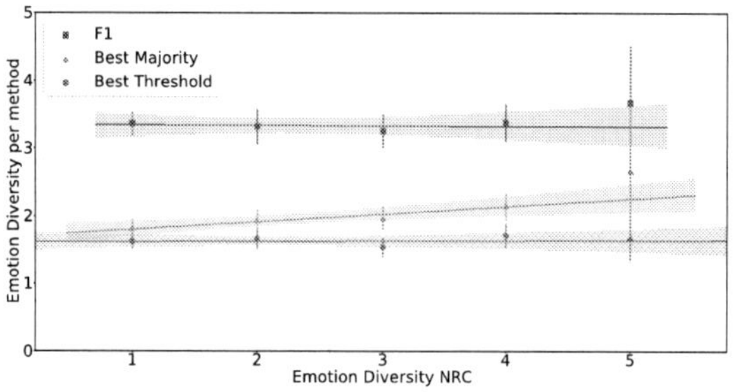

(c) 25%

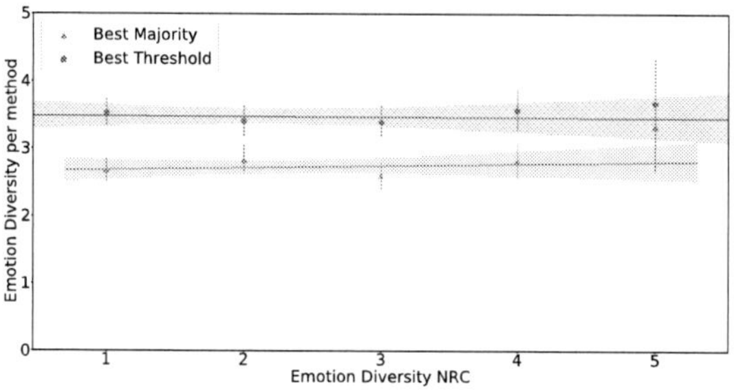

(d) 0%

Figure 10: Emotional Diversity of filtered methods compared to NRC for different objective term inclusion ratios

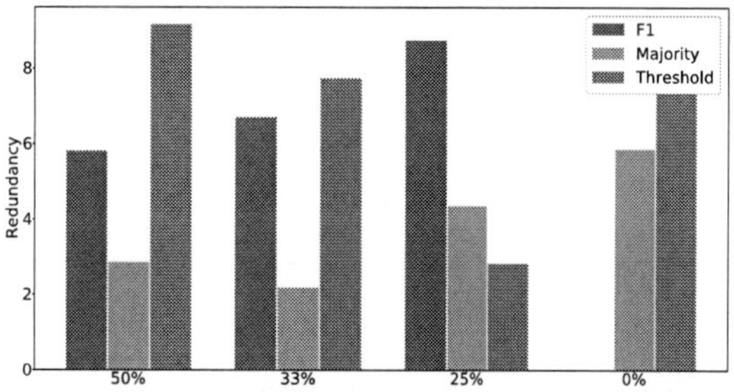

(a) Redundancy

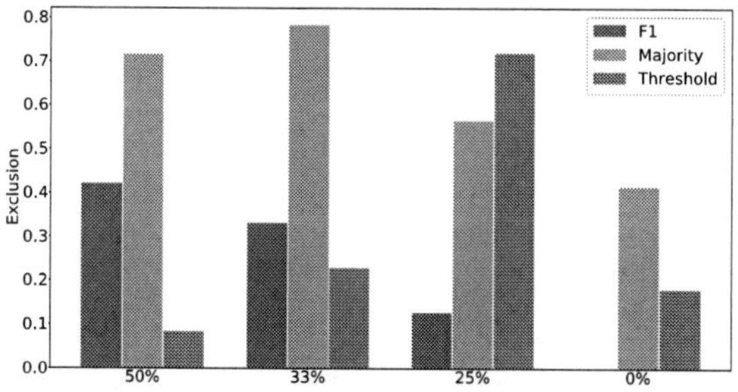

(b) Exclusion

Figure 11: Mean redundancy per term (a) and annotation exclusion (b) for different injection ratios

jective task has no ground truth(Aroyo and Welty, 2015) and contributors should not be judged by their subjective contributions to the task. We instead provide an objective evaluation process suited to subjective tasks.

Going forward, we intend to evaluate the performance of our method in tasks with varying design and also expand to subjective sentence labelling. Our proposed objective evaluation method can: be used in any domain with domain specific objective terms for evaluation, assess high quality contributors and preserve subjectivity by excluding contributors with low evaluation scores but retaining all the quality annotations.

7. Funding

This research was funded by Engineering and Physical Sciences Research Council grant number EP/M02315X/1: "From Human Data to Personal Experience".

8. Bibliographical References

Aker, A., El-Haj, M., Albakour, M.-D., Kruschwitz, U., et al. (2012). Assessing crowdsourcing quality through objective tasks. In *LREC*, pages 1456–1461. Citeseer.

Aroyo, L. and Welty, C. (2015). Truth is a lie: Crowd truth and the seven myths of human annotation. *AI Magazine*, 36(1):15–24.

Basile, V., Novielli, N., Croce, D., Barbieri, F., Nissim, M., and Patti, V. (2018). Sentiment polarity classification at evalita: Lessons learned and open challenges. *IEEE Transactions on Affective Computing*.

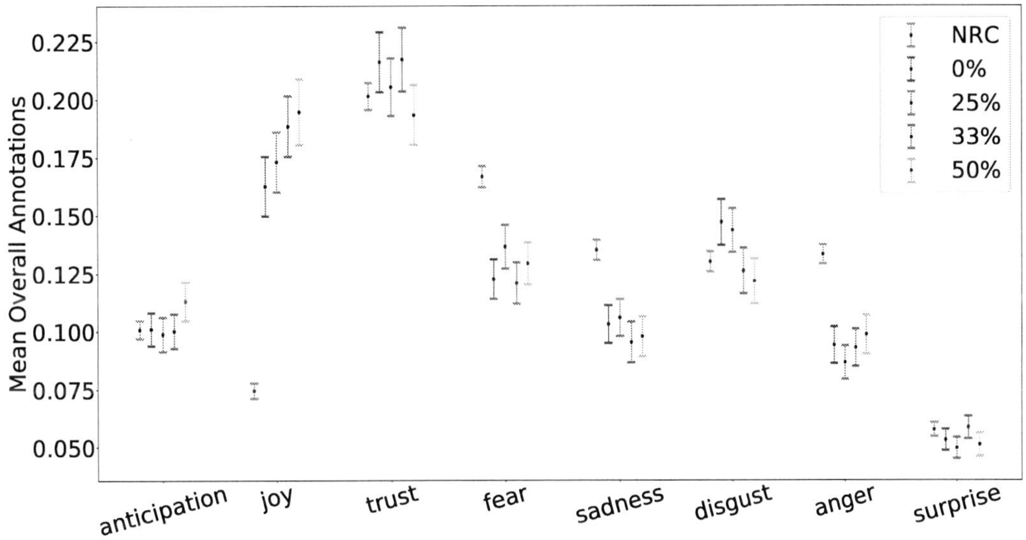

Figure 12: Mean Overall Annotations, for NRC and each injection ratio, with their respective standard error ranges

Brody, S., Keller, U., Degen, L., Cox, D. J., and Schächinger, H. (2004). Selective processing of food words during insulin-induced hypoglycemia in healthy humans. *Psychopharmacology*, 173(1-2):217–220.

Brosch, T., Pourtois, G., and Sander, D. (2010). The perception and categorisation of emotional stimuli: A review. *Cognition and emotion*, 24(3):377–400.

Budhi, G. S., Chiong, R., Hu, Z., Pranata, I., and Dhakal, S. (2018). Multi-pso based classifier selection and parameter optimisation for sentiment polarity prediction. In *2018 IEEE Conference on Big Data and Analytics (ICBDA)*, pages 68–73. IEEE.

Calefato, F., Lanubile, F., and Novielli, N. (2017). Emotxt: a toolkit for emotion recognition from text. In *2017 Seventh International Conference on Affective Computing and Intelligent Interaction Workshops and Demos (ACIIW)*, pages 79–80. IEEE.

Canetti, L., Bachar, E., and Berry, E. M. (2002). Food and emotion. *Behavioural processes*, 60(2):157–164.

Caselli, T., Sprugnoli, R., and Inel, O. (2016). Temporal information annotation: crowd vs. experts. In *Proceedings of the Tenth International Conference on Language Resources and Evaluation (LREC'16)*, pages 3502–3509.

Chamlertwat, W., Bhattarakosol, P., Rungkasiri, T., and Haruechaiyasak, C. (2012). Discovering consumer insight from twitter via sentiment analysis. *J. UCS*, 18(8):973–992.

Chaplin, T. M. (2015). Gender and emotion expression: A developmental contextual perspective. *Emotion Review*, 7(1):14–21.

Chaturvedi, I., Cambria, E., Welsch, R. E., and Herrera, F. (2018). Distinguishing between facts and opinions for sentiment analysis: Survey and challenges. *Information Fusion*, 44:65–77.

Diakopoulos, N. A. and Shamma, D. A. (2010). Characterizing debate performance via aggregated twitter sentiment. In *Proceedings of the SIGCHI Conference on Human Factors in Computing Systems*, pages 1195–1198. ACM.

Eickhoff, C. (2018). Cognitive biases in crowdsourcing. In *Proceedings of the Eleventh ACM International Conference on Web Search and Data Mining*, pages 162–170. ACM.

Ekman, P. and Friesen, W. V. (1971). Constants across cultures in the face and emotion. *Journal of personality and social psychology*, 17(2):124.

Ekman, P. and Keltner, D. (1997). Universal facial expressions of emotion. *Segerstrale U, P. Molnar P, eds. Nonverbal communication: Where nature meets culture*, pages 27–46.

Elfenbein, H. A. and Ambady, N. (2002). On the universality and cultural specificity of emotion recognition: a meta-analysis. *Psychological bulletin*, 128(2):203.

Elfenbein, H. A. and Luckman, E. A. (2016). 16 interpersonal accuracy in relation to culture and ethnicity. *The Social Psychology of Perceiving Others Accurately*, page 328.

Elfenbein, H. A. (2017). Emotional dialects in the language of emotion. *The science of facial expression*, pages 479–496.

Ellis, C. and Flaherty, M. G. (1992). An agenda for the interpretation of lived experience. *Investigating subjectivity: Research on lived experience*, pages 1–13.

Fernández-Gavilanes, M., Juncal-Martínez, J., García-Méndez, S., Costa-Montenegro, E., and González-Castaño, F. J. (2018). Creating emoji lexica from unsupervised sentiment analysis of their descriptions. *Expert Systems with Applications*, 103:74–91.

Finnerty, A., Kucherbaev, P., Tranquillini, S., and Convertino, G. (2013). Keep it simple: Reward and task design in crowdsourcing. In *Proceedings of the Biannual Conference of the Italian Chapter of SIGCHI*, page 14. ACM.

Ghosal, D., Akhtar, M. S., Ekbal, A., and Bhattacharyya, P. (2018). Deep ensemble model with the fusion of character, word and lexicon level information for emotion and sentiment prediction. In *International Conference on Neural Information Processing*, pages 162–174. Springer.

Ghosh, A., Li, G., Veale, T., Rosso, P., Shutova, E., Barnden, J., and Reyes, A. (2015). Semeval-2015 task 11: Sentiment analysis of figurative language in twitter. In *Proceedings of the 9th International Workshop on Semantic Evaluation (SemEval 2015)*, pages 470–478.

Gohier, B., Senior, C., Brittain, P., Lounes, N., El-Hage, W., Law, V., Phillips, M. L., and Surguladze, S. (2013). Gender differences in the sensitivity to negative stimuli: Cross-modal affective priming study. *European Psychiatry*, 28(2):74–80.

Haralabopoulos, G. and Simperl, E. (2017). Crowdsourcing for beyond polarity sentiment analysis a pure emotion lexicon. *arXiv preprint arXiv:1710.04203*.

Haralabopoulos, G., Wagner, C., McAuley, D., and Simperl, E. (2018). A multivalued emotion lexicon created and evaluated by the crowd. In *2018 Fifth International Conference on Social Networks Analysis, Management and Security (SNAMS)*, pages 355–362. IEEE.

Haralabopoulos, G., Wagner, C., McAuley, D., and Anagnostopoulos, I. (2019). Paid crowdsourcing, low income contributors, and subjectivity. In *IFIP International Conference on Artificial Intelligence Applications and Innovations*, pages 225–231. Springer.

Hazarika, D., Poria, S., Vij, P., Krishnamurthy, G., Cambria, E., and Zimmermann, R. (2018). Modeling inter-aspect dependencies for aspect-based sentiment analysis. In *Proceedings of the 2018 Conference of the North American Chapter of the Association for Computational Linguistics: Human Language Technologies, Volume 2 (Short Papers)*, volume 2, pages 266–270.

Hetmank, L. (2013). Components and functions of crowdsourcing systems-a systematic literature review. *Wirtschaftsinformatik*, 4:2013.

Howe, J. (2006). The rise of crowdsourcing. *Wired magazine*, 14(6):1–4.

Hutto, C. J. and Gilbert, E. (2014). Vader: A parsimonious rule-based model for sentiment analysis of social media text. In *Eighth international AAAI conference on weblogs and social media*.

Jonell, P., Oertel, C., Kontogiorgos, D., Beskow, J., and Gustafson, J. (2018). Crowdsourced multimodal corpora collection tool. In *The Eleventh International Conference on Language Resources and Evaluation (LREC 2018)*, pages 728–734.

Kang, D. and Park, Y. (2014). based measurement of customer satisfaction in mobile service: Sentiment analysis and vikor approach. *Expert Systems with Applications*, 41(4):1041–1050.

Keith, K. D. (2019). *Cross-cultural psychology: Contemporary themes and perspectives*. John Wiley & Sons.

Kiritchenko, S. and Mohammad, S. M. (2017). Capturing reliable fine-grained sentiment associations by crowdsourcing and best-worst scaling. *arXiv preprint arXiv:1712.01741*.

Kittur, A., Chi, E. H., and Suh, B. (2008). Crowdsourcing user studies with mechanical turk. In *Proceedings of the SIGCHI conference on human factors in computing systems*, pages 453–456. ACM.

Knapp, M. L., Hall, J. A., and Horgan, T. G. (2013). *Nonverbal communication in human interaction*. Cengage Learning.

Koltsova, O. Y., Alexeeva, S., and Kolcov, S. (2016). An opinion word lexicon and a training dataset for russian sentiment analysis of social media. *Computational Linguistics and Intellectual Technologies: Materials of DIALOGUE 2016 (Moscow)*, pages 277–287.

Lau, R. Y., Li, C., and Liao, S. S. (2014). Social analytics: Learning fuzzy product ontologies for aspect-oriented sentiment analysis. *Decision Support Systems*, 65:80–94.

Lauka, A., McCoy, J., and Firat, R. B. (2018). Mass partisan polarization: Measuring a relational concept. *American behavioral scientist*, 62(1):107–126.

Li, G., Wang, J., Zheng, Y., Fan, J., and Franklin, M. J. (2018). Crowdsourcing background. In *Crowdsourced Data Management*, pages 11–20. Springer.

Luhrmann, T. M. (2006). Subjectivity. *Anthropological Theory*, 6(3):345–361.

Masuda, T., Gonzalez, R., Kwan, L., and Nisbett, R. E. (2008). Culture and aesthetic preference: Comparing the attention to context of east asians and americans. *Personality and Social Psychology Bulletin*, 34(9):1260–1275.

Matsumoto, D., Hwang, H. C., and Frank, M. G. (2013). Emotional language and political aggression. *Journal of Language and Social Psychology*, 32(4):452–468.

Maynard, D. and Bontcheva, K. (2016). Challenges of evaluating sentiment analysis tools on social media. In *Proceedings of the Tenth International Conference on Language Resources and Evaluation (LREC 2016)*, pages 1142–1148. LREC.

Miao, H., Liu, R., Gao, S., Zhou, X., and He, X. (2018). End-to-end deep memory network for visual-textual sentiment analysis. In *2018 International Conference on Network Infrastructure and Digital Content (IC-NIDC)*, pages 399–403. IEEE.

Mihalcea, R., Banea, C., and Wiebe, J. (2007). Learning multilingual subjective language via cross-lingual projections. In *Proceedings of the 45th annual meeting of the association of computational linguistics*, pages 976–983.

Mohammad, S. M., Kiritchenko, S., and Zhu, X. (2013). Nrc-canada: Building the state-of-the-art in sentiment analysis of tweets. *arXiv preprint arXiv:1308.6242*.

O'Leary, D. E. (2016). On the relationship between number of votes and sentiment in crowdsourcing ideas and comments for innovation: A case study of canada's digital compass. *Decision Support Systems*, 88:28–37.

Öztürk, N. and Ayvaz, S. (2018). Sentiment analysis on

twitter: A text mining approach to the syrian refugee crisis. *Telematics and Informatics*, 35(1):136–147.

Palan, S. and Schitter, C. (2018). Prolific. ac—a subject pool for online experiments. *Journal of Behavioral and Experimental Finance*, 17:22–27.

Peer, E., Brandimarte, L., Samat, S., and Acquisti, A. (2017). Beyond the turk: Alternative platforms for crowdsourcing behavioral research. *Journal of Experimental Social Psychology*, 70:153–163.

Pessoa, L. and Adolphs, R. (2010). Emotion processing and the amygdala: from a'low road'to'many roads' of evaluating biological significance. *Nature reviews neuroscience*, 11(11):773.

Plutchik, R. (1980). A general psychoevolutionary theory of emotion. In *Theories of emotion*, pages 3–33. Elsevier.

Prabowo, R. and Thelwall, M. (2009). Sentiment analysis: A combined approach. *Journal of Informetrics*, 3(2):143–157.

Ranco, G., Aleksovski, D., Caldarelli, G., Grčar, M., and Mozetič, I. (2015). The effects of twitter sentiment on stock price returns. *PloS one*, 10(9):e0138441.

Reidy, D. E., Brookmeyer, K. A., Gentile, B., Berke, D. S., and Zeichner, A. (2016). Gender role discrepancy stress, high-risk sexual behavior, and sexually transmitted disease. *Archives of sexual behavior*, 45(2):459–465.

Rouder, J., Morey, R., and Wagenmakers, E.-J. (2016). The interplay between subjectivity, statistical practice, and psychological science. *Collabra: Psychology*, 2(1).

Schouten, K., Van Der Weijde, O., Frasincar, F., and Dekker, R. (2018). Supervised and unsupervised aspect category detection for sentiment analysis with co-occurrence data. *IEEE transactions on cybernetics*, 48(4):1263–1275.

Schumaker, R. P., Jarmoszko, A. T., and Labedz Jr, C. S. (2016). Predicting wins and spread in the premier league using a sentiment analysis of twitter. *Decision Support Systems*, 88:76–84.

Semnani-Azad, Z. and Adair, W. L. (2013). Watch your tone… relational paralinguistic messages in negotiation: The case of east and west. *International Studies of Management & Organization*, 43(4):64–89.

Sharma, S. and Chakraverty, S. (2018). An approach to track context switches in sentiment analysis. In *Progress in Advanced Computing and Intelligent Engineering*, pages 273–282. Springer.

Silvers, J. A., Insel, C., Powers, A., Franz, P., Helion, C., Martin, R. E., Weber, J., Mischel, W., Casey, B., and Ochsner, K. N. (2016). vlpfc–vmpfc–amygdala interactions underlie age-related differences in cognitive regulation of emotion. *Cerebral Cortex*, 27(7):3502–3514.

Smith, A. K. and Elias, L. J. (2018). Native reading direction modulates eye movements during aesthetic preference and brightness judgments. *Psychology of Aesthetics, Creativity, and the Arts*.

Smith, J. A. (2015). *Qualitative psychology: A practical guide to research methods*. Sage.

Starr, M. S. and Rayner, K. (2001). Eye movements during reading: Some current controversies. *Trends in cognitive sciences*, 5(4):156–163.

Tang, D., Qin, B., and Liu, T. (2015). Document modeling with gated recurrent neural network for sentiment classification. In *Proceedings of the 2015 conference on empirical methods in natural language processing*, pages 1422–1432.

Teo, T. (2018). Homo neoliberalus: From personality to forms of subjectivity. *Theory & Psychology*, 28(5):581–599.

Valdivia, A., Luzón, M. V., Cambria, E., and Herrera, F. (2018). Consensus vote models for detecting and filtering neutrality in sentiment analysis. *Information Fusion*, 44:126–135.

White, S. J., Warrington, K. L., McGowan, V. A., and Paterson, K. B. (2015). Eye movements during reading and topic scanning: Effects of word frequency. *Journal of Experimental Psychology: Human Perception and Performance*, 41(1):233.

Yao, Y.-W., Liu, L., Ma, S.-S., Shi, X.-H., Zhou, N., Zhang, J.-T., and Potenza, M. N. (2017). Functional and structural neural alterations in internet gaming disorder: A systematic review and meta-analysis. *Neuroscience & Biobehavioral Reviews*, 83:313–324.

Yoshino, K., Ishikawa, Y., Mizukami, M., Suzuki, Y., Sakti, S., and Nakamura, S. (2018). Dialogue scenario collection of persuasive dialogue with emotional expressions via crowdsourcing. In *Proceedings of the Eleventh International Conference on Language Resources and Evaluation (LREC 2018)*.

Yue, L., Chen, W., Li, X., Zuo, W., and Yin, M. (2018). A survey of sentiment analysis in social media. *Knowledge and Information Systems*, pages 1–47.

Zamil, A. A. A., Hasan, S., Baki, S. M. J., Adam, J. M., and Zaman, I. (2019). Emotion detection from speech signals using voting mechanism on classified frames. In *2019 International Conference on Robotics, Electrical and Signal Processing Techniques (ICREST)*, pages 281–285. IEEE.

Zhao, W., Guan, Z., Chen, L., He, X., Cai, D., Wang, B., and Wang, Q. (2018). Weakly-supervised deep embedding for product review sentiment analysis. *IEEE Transactions on Knowledge and Data Engineering*, 30(1):185–197.

Proceedings of the LREC 2020 Workshop "Citizen Linguistics in Language Resource Development", pages 26–34
Language Resources and Evaluation Conference (LREC 2020), Marseille, 11–16 May 2020

Speaking Outside the Box: Exploring the Benefits of Unconstrained Input in Crowdsourcing and Citizen Science Platforms

Jon Chamberlain[a], Udo Kruschwitz[b] & Massimo Poesio[c]
[a] University of Essex, Wivenhoe Park, Colchester, Essex UK. jchamb@essex.ac.uk
[b] Universität Regensburg, 93040 Regensburg, Germany. udo.kruschwitz@ur.de
[c] Queen Mary University of London, Mile End Rd, Bethnal Green, London UK. m.poesio@qmul.ac.uk

Abstract

Crowdsourcing approaches provide a difficult design challenge for developers. There is a trade-off between the efficiency of the task to be done and the reward given to the user for participating, whether it be altruism, social enhancement, entertainment or money. This paper explores how crowdsourcing and citizen science systems collect data and complete tasks, illustrated by a case study from the online language game-with-a-purpose Phrase Detectives. The game was originally developed to be a constrained interface to prevent player collusion, but subsequently benefited from posthoc analysis of over 76k unconstrained inputs from users. Understanding the interface design and task deconstruction are critical for enabling users to participate in such systems and the paper concludes with a discussion of the idea that social networks can be viewed as form of citizen science platform with both constrained and unconstrained inputs making for a highly complex dataset.

Keywords: crowdsourcing, citizen science, unconstrained, interface design, verbatim, input type, natural language interface

1. Introduction

The popularity of crowdsourcing approaches in recent years, encompassing everything from microworking to citizen science and all systems in between, has proved a difficult design challenge for system developers. Primarily such systems are designed to collect, label or in some way engage human participants in solving problems that cannot be done computationally (and to help train systems to perform tasks better). There is a trade-off between the efficiency of the task to be done and the reward given to the user for participating, whether it be altruism, social enhancement, entertainment or money. This trade-off is key to ensuring systems work for both the *requester* (the party that wants the task to be completed) and the *worker* (the party that does the task). From the point of view of the requester, the most efficient way to collect the data required is to constrain the worker to a pre-defined set of responses that can be easily processed, aggregated and analysed, with poor performing users identified against a gold standard and excluded from contributing. However, from the point of view of the worker, the pre-defined set of solution options may be ambiguous and they may not be able to fully express their intent and solution to the task.

In a toy example, consider a theatre booking website that requires a user to enter a date to book a ticket for a show. The *requester* (the theatre) requires a date (the task) to be entered into the system so it can be matched to a date in the database of remaining tickets for sale and automatically processed to issue the ticket. Hence, a set of predefined dropdown select boxes are offered to the user on the booking form (or an interactive calendar selection popup). The result is that the user can only enter a date that the system can recognise. However, the user may find that the constrained input does not allow them to query the system in a way they would find natural, for example, they may wish to use natural language to express their intent ('tomorrow', 'next Monday', or 'the first Saturday in June') or provide an ambiguous answer more aligned to their intention, e.g., 'next Saturday but if fully booked then the Saturday after'. In the trade-off between precise booking and user experience, the former approach is more commonly used than the latter, although the rise of chatbots for a more personalised booking experience may indicate the beginnings of a paradigm shift to a more human-centred interface (Elsholz et al., 2019).

This paper explores how crowdsourcing and citizen science systems collect data and complete tasks by characterising the type of task and style of interface used in popular systems (Section 2). Section 3 presents a case study of research from the online language game-with-a-purpose *Phrase Detectives*, originally developed to be a constrained interface to prevent player collusion, but subsequently benefited from posthoc analysis of unconstrained input from users. Section 4 generalises further how the interface design and task deconstruction are critical for enabling users to participate in such systems and explores the idea that social networks can be viewed as form of citizen science platform with both constrained and unconstrained inputs making for a highly complex dataset.

2. Related Work

Crowdsourcing (Howe, 2008) has become ubiquitous in systems where tasks need to be completed by human workers that are too difficult for computers to perform accurately. This section provides a brief overview of the most common types of crowdsourcing systems and characterises them by how the task is processed.

Peer production Peer production is a way of completing tasks that relies on self-organising communities of individuals in which effort is coordinated towards a shared outcome (Benkler and Nissenbaum, 2006). The willingness of Web users to collaborate in peer production can be seen in the creation of resources such as Wikipedia. English Wikipedia numbers (as of Feb 2020) over 6M articles, contributed to by over 38M users.[1] The key aspects that make peer production so successful are the openness of the data resource being created and the transparency of the community that is creating it (Lakhani et al., 2007; Dabbish et al., 2014).

People who contribute information to Wikipedia are motivated by personal reasons such as the desire to make a particular page accurate, or the pride in one's knowledge in a certain subject matter (Yang and Lai, 2010). This motivation is also behind the success of **citizen science** projects, such as the *Zooniverse* collection of projects[2], in which the scientific research is conducted mainly by amateur scientists and members of the public (Clery, 2011). The costs of ambitious data annotation tasks are also kept to a minimum, with expert annotators only required to validate a small portion of the data (which is also likely to be the data of most interest them).

Question answering systems attempt to learn how to answer a question automatically from a human, either from structured data or from processing natural language of existing conversations and dialogue. Here we are more interested in **Community Question Answering (cQA)**, in which the crowd is the system that attempts to answer the question through natural language. Examples of cQA are sites such as StackOveflow[3] and Yahoo Answers.[4] Detailed schemas (Bunt et al., 2012) and rich feature sets (Agichtein et al., 2008) have been used to describe cQA dialogue and progress has been made to analyse this source of data automatically (Su et al., 2007).

Microworking Amazon Mechanical Turk[5] pioneered microwork crowdsourcing by using the Web as a way of reaching large numbers of workers (often referred to as turkers) who get paid to complete small items of work called human intelligence tasks (HITs). This is typically very little, in the order of 0.01 to 0.20 US$ per HIT. A reported advantage of microworking is that the work is completed very fast. It is not uncommon for a HIT to be completed in minutes, but this is usually for simple tasks. In the case of more complex tasks, or tasks in which the worker needs to be more skilled, e.g. translating a sentence in an uncommon language, it can take much longer (Novotney and Callison-Burch, 2010). Microwork crowdsourcing is becoming a standard way of creating small-scale resources, but is prohibitively expensive to create large-scale resources.

Gaming and games-with-a-purpose Generally speaking, a game-based crowdsourcing approach uses entertainment rather than financial payment to motivate participation. The approach is motivated by the observation that every year people spend billions of hours playing games on the Web (von Ahn, 2006). A game-with-a-purpose (GWAP) can come in many forms; they tend to be graphically rich, with simple interfaces, and give the player an experience of progression through the game by scoring points, being assigned levels and recognising their effort. Systems are required to control the behaviour of players: to encourage them to concentrate on the tasks and to discourage them from malicious behaviour.

Social computing and social networks Social computing has been described as 'applications and services that facilitate collective action and social interaction online with rich exchange of multimedia information and evolution of aggregate knowledge' (Parameswaran and Whinston, 2007). It encompasses technologies that enable communities to gather online such as blogs, forums and social networks, although the purpose is largely not to solve problems directly. The open dialogue and self-organising structure of social networks[6] allow many types of human interaction, but here we are most interested in the idea of community problem solving, in which one user creates a task and the community solves it for them. As social networks mature the software is utilised in different ways, with decentralised and unevenly-distributed organisation of content, similar to how Wikipedia users create pages of dictionary content. Increasingly, social networks are being used to organise data, to pose problems, and to connect people who may have solutions that can be contributed in a simple and socially-convenient fashion. Facebook has been used as a way of connecting professional scientists and amateur enthusiasts with considerable success (Sidlauskas et al., 2011; Gonella et al., 2015). However, there are drawbacks with this method of knowledge sharing and problem solving: data may be lost to people interested in them in the future and they are often not accessible in a simple way, for example, with a search engine.

2.1. Features of crowdsourcing tasks

Crowdsourcing approaches can be distinguished by features related to the task. To clarify why these features apply to a particular approach an exemplar system is chosen for the approach that is perhaps the most prevalent or successful: Manual annotation is considered the benchmark where the task is completed by an expert; *GalaxyZoo* represents citizen science (although a detailed typology for citizen science projects also exists (Wiggins and Crowston, 2011)); *StackOverflow* represents Community Question Answering (cQA); *Wikipedia*'s main website is an example of a wiki-type approach; for microworking, *Amazon Mechanical Turk* is used; for GWAPs, the *ESP game* is used; and finally for social networks, *Facebook* itself is considered (rather than a system implemented on the platform).

The type of task that is presented covers the dimension of *how* the problem gets solved (Malone et al., 2009). One of the important features for distinguishing individual projects (rather than the approach) is to look at **task difficulty**, either as a function of the task (*routine, complex* or *creative* (Schenk and Guittard, 2011)) or as a function of worker *cognitive load* (Quinn and Bederson, 2011). Also useful for distinguishing between projects is the **centrality** of the

[1] `http://meta.wikimedia.org/wiki/List_of_Wikipedias`, accessed 18/2/2020.

[2] `https://www.zooniverse.org`

[3] `http://stackoverflow.com`

[4] `https://uk.answers.yahoo.com`

[5] `http://www.mturk.com`

[6] For the context of this paper we define a social network as the platform for communication, rather than a system deployed on the platform or the social network structure itself.

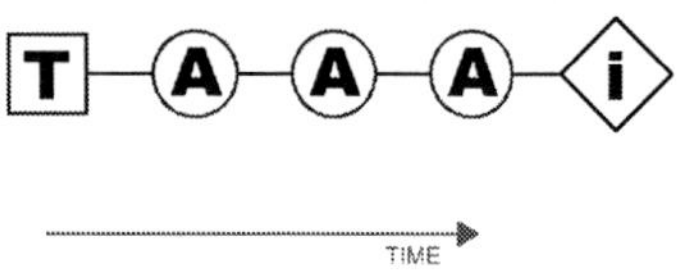

Figure 1: A task T can be completed in series in which each annotation A is dependent on the one before and leads to one interpretation i (Wikipedia, cQA and social networks).

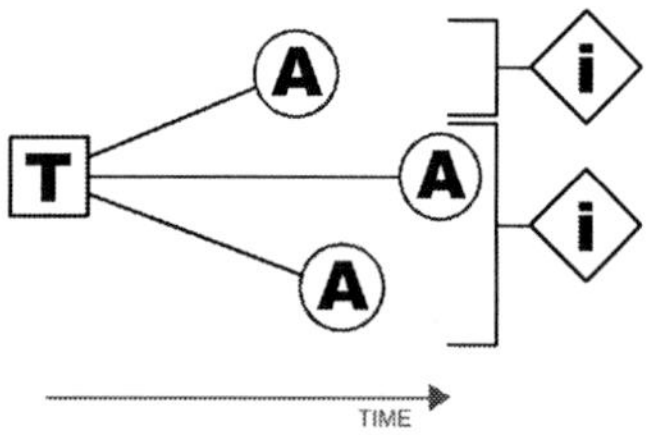

Figure 2: T can also be completed in parallel in which annotations can be entered simultaneously leading to multiple interpretations that require post-processing for a final output (microworking, GWAPs and manual annotation).

crowdsourcing in the system, i.e. is the crowdsourcing *core* to the system, such as creating content in Wikipedia, or is it *peripheral* such as rating articles (Organisciak and Twidale, 2015). Task features are discussed below and summarised in Table 1.

Input constraint Whilst data are often structured, mainly to allow them to be input into the system, the contributions may not necessarily be. Crowdsourcing typically constrains workers to enter a restricted range of inputs via radio buttons and dropdown lists, whereas social networks and peer production allow unconstrained text input that requires post-processing. Some tasks require annotations to be aligned to an ontology and this provides structure; however, spelling mistakes and ambiguity can cause errors. Along with unconstrained page creation, Wikipedia allows for semi-constrained input through summary boxes on each page. The choice of input constraint may be driven by a further facet of whether the answers to the task need to be *objective* or *subjective* (Organisciak and Twidale, 2015).

Input order The timing of the presentation of the tasks is dependent on the system and, generally speaking, will determine how fast a system can produce an output for a task. In the case of Wikipedia, cQA and social networks, a task is added and each worker contributes in series, i.e. each contribution is dependent on the previous contributions in the way a Wikipedia page is developed or a conversation thread flows (see Figure 1). Workers on Wikipedia can edit and overwrite the text on a page. This 'last edit wins' approach is fundamental to building the content; however, contentious subjects may cause 'edit wars' and pages may become locked to prevent future editing.
In order to increase crowdsourcing efficiency, some systems allow tasks to be completed in parallel, i.e. multiple workers annotate different tasks at different times meaning that not all tasks will be completed in the same amount of time (see Figure 2). Parallel tasks are common in microworking, GWAPs and citizen science. Expert manual annotation can be completed both in series or in parallel.
A wider, systematic view of task order would be to view the system's **procedural order** and how the worker interacts with system inputs and responses from the crowd (Organisciak and Twidale, 2015; Chamberlain and O'Reilly, 2014).

Validation Quality control of a system is a feature of most typologies of crowdsourcing and can be used to distinguish between different projects (Quinn and Bederson, 2011; Das and Vukovic, 2011); however, it creates a large and complex facet group that is beyond the scope of what is required here. In this context, it is the reviewers of the annotations supplied by the workers that is of interest.
Validation on some level occurs after annotations have been applied to the data; the issue is whether those validations are part of the process that the workers are involved in or whether it is a form of checking from the requester to ensure that a sample of the annotations are of a high enough quality. It is typically the case for requesters to check a sample of annotations with experts, microworking and citizen science. In systems such as Wikipedia, social networks and cQA, the checking and validation of all answers is done by the workers themselves. GWAP annotations are typically validated by the requester; however, an increasing proportion of games are using validation as an additional worker task to reduce the workload for the requester (Chamberlain et al., 2018).

3. Case Study: Phrase Detectives

Phrase Detectives[7] is an online citizen science game designed to collect data about English anaphoric coreference (Chamberlain et al., 2008; Poesio et al., 2013).[8]

3.1. Constrained input

The game uses two styles of constrained text annotation for players to complete the linguistic task. Initially text is presented in **Annotation Mode** (called Name the Culprit in the

[7] http://www.phrasedetectives.com

[8] Anaphoric coreference is a type of linguistic reference where one expression depends on another referential element. An example would be the relation between the entity *'Jon'* and the pronoun *'his'* in the text *'Jon rode his bike to school.'*

Table 1: A table showing task features, including whether the input is constrained, in what order it can be entered and who checks it.

	Input constraint	Input order	Validation by
Expert annotation	Constrained	Both	Requester
Peer production: Citizen science	Constrained	Parallel	Requester
GWAP	Constrained	Parallel	Both
Microworking	Constrained	Parallel	Requester
Peer production: Wikipedia	Unconstrained	Series	Worker
Peer production: cQA	Unconstrained	Series	Worker
Social Networks	Unconstrained	Series	Worker

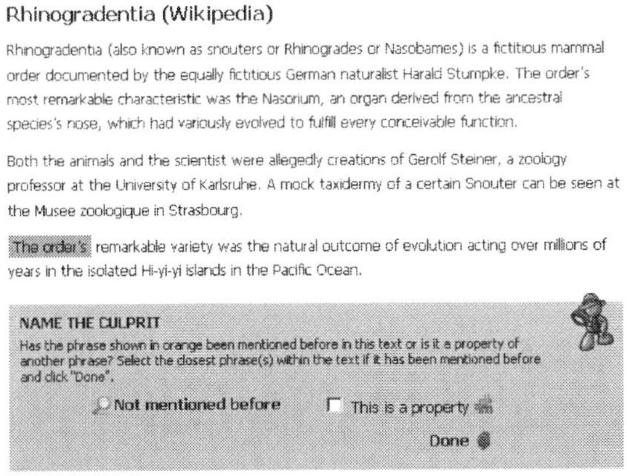

Figure 3: Constrained input (Annotation Mode) for players of *Phrase Detectives*.

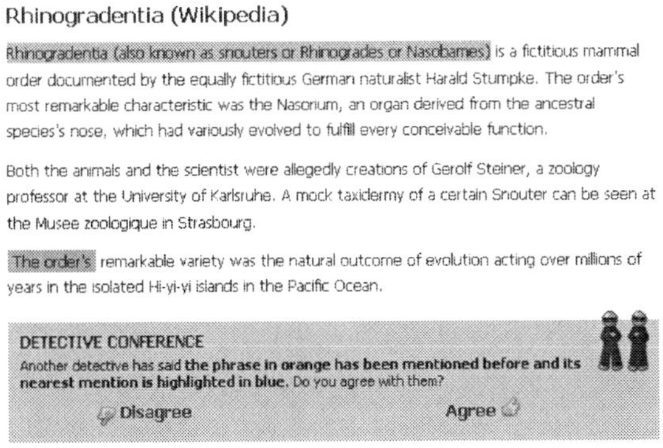

Figure 4: Constrained input (Validation Mode) for players of *Phrase Detectives*.

Figure 5: Unconstrained input options during Annotation Mode for players of *Phrase Detectives*.

game, see Figure 3). This is a traditional annotation method in which the player makes an **interpretation** (annotation decision) about a highlighted **markable** (section of text). Markables are identified using pre-processing and are a defined set of options within the context of text shown to the player. Players can select multiple markable antecedents if they believe the anaphor is plural. Players can also select options without selecting a markable, e.g., to indicate the markable has not been mentioned before in the text. Although the number of possible interpretations players could enter is very large, in practice players converge on sensible interpretations for the task.

If different players enter different interpretations for a markable then each interpretation is presented to more players in a constrained, binary task **Validation Mode** (called Detectives Conference in the game, see Figure 4). The players in Validation Mode have to agree or disagree with the interpretation. If they disagree, their decision is recorded and they are then presented with Annotation Mode for the same markable.

This method of data collection was originally designed into the game to reduce collusion between the players during a gameplay (von Ahn and Dabbish, 2008), whilst rewarding players who made the effort to put in good quality solutions to the task.

3.2. Unconstrained input

During early prototyping of the game it became clear that players were encountering tasks they could not complete with the set of constrained inputs on offer. The most com-

mon at the time was to indicate that the pre-processing of markables contained an error, either in the boundary of the tokens or that the markable was not a noun phrase. For this reason an unconstrained input option was added to Annotation Mode (also accessible from Validation Mode by disagreeing with the interpretation) to allow players to indicate that something was wrong or what they couldn't express with the limited set of options available in the game (see Figure 5).
For player convenience, several 'skip' buttons were shown that allow the player to quickly skip the task but also to indicate why in a single click. By clicking a skip option, a 'skip' event is created in the database; if the skip option had a reason a 'comment' event was additionally created in the database. The full range of unconstrained player responses were:

1. **Comment on this phrase** A freetext comment that when submitted does not conclude the task, i.e, the player can also add a solution or skip;
2. **Skip - error in the text** Skip the task because the markable has an error;
3. **Skip this one** Skip the task but not provide a reason why (no comment is created);
4. **Skip - closest phrase no longer visible** Skip the task because the player has seen the solution in a previous part of the text that is no longer accessible;
5. **Skip - closest phrase can't be selected** Skip the task because although the phrase the player wants to select is in the text it is not one of the predefined markables (and this also occurs when markables are embedded in larger markables, such as in the case of apposition.);
6. **Skip - this is discourse deixis** Discourse deixis is a relatively easy linguistic phenomenon for players to identify but there was no way to mark it as a solution to the task (this was added due to player requests);
7. **Skip - this is a quantifier** As above, players could easily identify solutions to tasks that were quantifiers but did not have the option to mark it as such (again, added due to player requests).

3.3. Consolidation of Unconstrained Input

The constrained inputs from the players have been analysed in several ways, initially using majority voting for a collective decision making (Chamberlain et al., 2018), then with more advanced modelling through Mention-Pair Analysis (MPA) (Poesio et al., 2019). However, these techniques did not make use of any of the unconstrained data collected from the players.
In order to make the unconstrained data into a more useful form it was consolidated semi-automatically (see Figure 6) and included in the corpora released for further research (Poesio et al., 2019). Each comment was classified initially by the player (by the type of skip they select) and then by an administrator. The administrator can then take action in relation to the comment, e.g., correcting markable boundaries (which is flagged in a checkbox) and/or publish the comment with the corpus (in fact, all comments are published in the corpus, this flag is an indication that the administrator thought the comment was useful). Links to other comments on the same markable can be seen so they can all be dealt with at the same time.

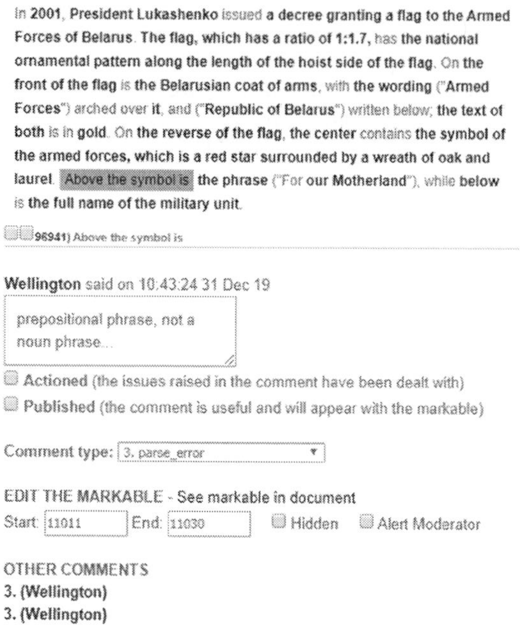

Figure 6: Admin screen in *Phrase Detectives* that allows reviewers to process the unconstrained input of players.

Table 2: A breakdown of comments received in *Phrase Detectives*, in which *Skip* relates to the type of skip made in the interface.

Classification	Skip	Comments
Not selectable	[5]	31,846
Out of context window	[4]	21,732
Parse error	[2]	15,707
Discourse deixis	[6]	328
Ambiguous		49
Non-referring		24
Nearest mention embedding		237
Bridging reference		11
Quantifier	[7]	50
Unclassified		6,899
TOTAL		76,883

3.4. Data

As of 18 Feb 2020 there were 114,353 skips and 76,883 comments added by players of *Phrase Detectives*, in comparison to 3,179,850 annotation and 1,420,191 validation decisions, from a total of 60,965 players working on 843 documents. A breakdown of each comment type can been seen in Table 2. The ratio of skips to annotations per player is approx. 4% and comments to annotations is approx. 2%.

3.5. Uses of Unconstrained Data

The most immediate use of the skip and comment functionality in *Phrase Detectives* was to elicit feedback from the players regarding errors in the corpus and interface design problems. The skip data was incorporated as a way to determine whether players should stop being given a markable because there was something wrong with it. Comments regarding pre-processing errors, markables not being available to be selected or beyond the piece of text visible to the player account for the majority of comments from users.

The way players provided unconstrained input to the system in this way enabled the development of specific functionality for a small group of high performing players who wanted to provide more detailed solutions to the tasks. For example, these players frequently used the comment field to indicate markables where discourse deixis or quantifier was the most appropriate interpretation by commenting 'DD' and 'QQ' respectively. By creating their own annotation input (likely based on other annotation schemes) the players were providing a level of input to the system that was beyond what the interface was designed for. Based on these comments, additional skip types were added to the interface to enable these players to provide this input faster during their gameplay.

The verbatim comments allowed us to understand some interesting and ambiguous phenomena encountered in the data that could only have been understood with posthoc analysis. Issues of context, plural union and separation, bridging, naming conventions, temporal revelations, measurements, dates, and generality/specificity were all addressed using the comment functionality giving administrators a unique understanding into why player decision making diverged from consensus.

In addition to manual posthoc analysis, the skips and comments are being developed into future versions of the MPA algorithm (Poesio et al., 2019), used to detect emergent communities of players who respond to stimuli in different ways. Anaphoric resolvers that analyse complex, ambiguous datasets (like those created by *Phrase Detectives*) using neural network approaches may perform better due to the richness of multi-dimensional data at their disposal.

3.6. A Fully Unconstrained Interface?

To conclude our case study of how unconstrained input was gathered from players of *Phrase Detectives*, we report on two efforts that were made to create interfaces that were entirely unconstrained (due to the platform limitations, rather than design requirements).

An attempt was made to emulate the anaphoric coreference task in *Phrase Detectives* using microworking; however, this proved to be very difficult as the users were restricted to entering an imprecise text notation, for example having to write *DO line 2 "the door"* for a highlighted markable or using two inputs to select the class of relation and where the antecedent is (see Figure 7).

In the hope of leveraging the social networking platform Facebook's community of users, an unconstrained version of the task was presented through a user group called Anaphor from your Elbow, a contraction of the question *Do you know your anaphor from your elbow?*, (see Figure 8) where an image of the language task was posted and the users commented on the image as to where the antecedent was in the text (in the same way as above).

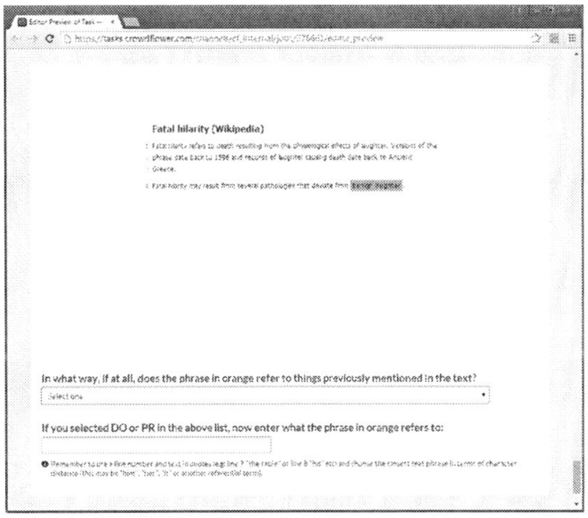

Figure 7: Screenshot of the anaphoric coreference task presented in Crowdflower.

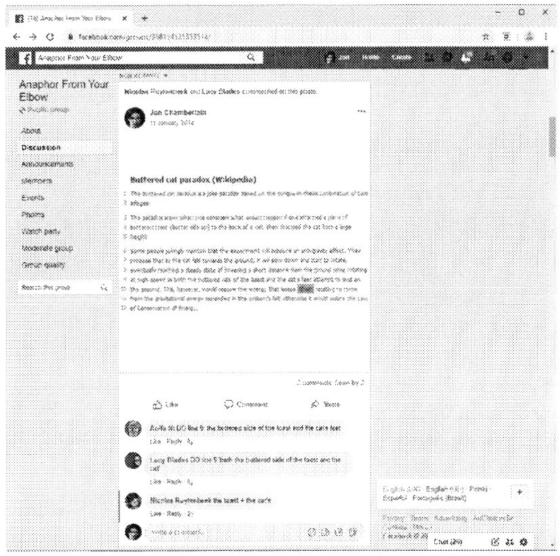

Figure 8: Screenshot of the Anaphora from your Elbow Facebook group where the unconstrained anaphoric coreference task was presented.

Given the difficulties of pre-formatting the text as an image, as well as post-processing the unconstrained comments from the users, these experiments were abandoned in favour of developing the constrained game interface of *Phrase Detectives* to incorporate more unconstrained input from players.

4. Discussion

4.1. Interface Design

The design of the interface will determine how successfully the user can contribute data to a crowdsourcing system. In *Phrase Detectives* the player is constrained to a set of predefined options to make annotations, with freetext comments allowed (although this is not the usual mode of interaction with the game). The pre-processing of text allows the interface to be constrained in this way, but is subject to errors in pre-processing that must also be fixed.

The interface of microworking sites is also predefined and presents limitations that constitute an important issue for some tasks, for example, in annotating noun compound relations using a large taxonomy (Tratz and Hovy, 2010). In a word sense disambiguation task, considerable redesigns were required to get satisfactory results (Hong and Baker, 2011). These examples show how difficult it is to design tasks for crowdsourcing within a predefined system. The design of social network interfaces is dictated by the owners of the platforms, rather than the requester or the community of users and crowdsourcing efforts may be in conflict with other revenue-generating activities such as advertising.

The interface design has an impact on the speed at which players can complete tasks, with clicking being faster than typing. A design decision to use radio buttons or freetext boxes can have a significant impact on performance (Aker et al., 2012) and response times (Chamberlain and O'Reilly, 2014). Errors in the data constitute wasted effort and should be dealt with by bug testing the system rather than post-processing.

4.2. Task Difficulty

Crowdsourcing and citizen science can produce high-quality work from users, comparable to work of an expert, if communities of users can be found to do the task. The task of anaphoric coreference as used in *Phrase Detectives* is not simple and, although the majority of tasks were not hard, it is the uncommon difficult tasks that require the power of human computation. A less-constrained environment allows these difficult tasks to be solved in more organic ways compared to a fully constrained system.

There is a clear difference in quality when we look at the difficulty of the tasks in *Phrase Detectives*. Looking separately at the agreement on each class of markable annotation, we observe near-expert quality for the simple task of identifying discourse-new (DN) markables, whereas discourse-old (DO) markables are more difficult (Chamberlain et al., 2016). This demonstrates that quality is not only affected by player motivation and interface design but also by the inherent difficulty of the task. Users need to be motivated to rise to the challenge of difficult tasks and this is when financial incentives may prove to be too expensive on a large scale.

The quality of the work produced by microworking, with appropriate post-processing, seems sufficient to train and evaluate statistical translation or transcription systems (Callison-Burch and Dredze, 2010; Marge et al., 2010). However, it varies from one task to another according to the defining parameters. Unsurprisingly, workers seem to have difficulty performing complex tasks, such as the evaluation of summarisation systems (Gillick and Liu, 2010).

A task may be difficult for several reasons: the correct answer is difficult, but not impossible, to determine; the true interpretation is a difficult type of solution to determine; or that the answer is genuinely ambiguous and there is more than one plausible solution. The latter tasks can be rare, but are of the most interest to computational linguists and machine learning algorithms. In these cases the users need to have a thorough understanding of how to add their solutions and an unconstrained input option would capture data beyond what the interface may have been designed for; however, automatically processing these cases can be difficult.

4.3. Citizen Science on Social Networks

Social networking sites such as Facebook, Twitter and Instagram have all been used for conducting citizens science activities. Harnessing the collective intelligence of communities on social networks is not straightforward, but the rewards are high. If a suitable community can be found to align with the task of the requester and the data can be extracted from the network, it has shown to be a useful type of crowdsourcing approach. Aggregating the social network data in a similar way to crowdsourcing (Chamberlain, 2014) will allow the automatic extraction of knowledge and sophisticated crowd aggregation techniques (Raykar et al., 2010) can be used to gauge the confidence of data extracted from threads on a large scale.

A validation model is intuitive to users and features in some form on most social network platforms. Typically a 'like' or 'upvote' button can be found on messages and replies, allowing the community to show favour for particular solutions, and this method has been shown to be effective and efficient in experimental work (Chamberlain, 2014). Other forms of voting exist, such as full validation (like and dislike) or graded voting (using a five star vote system) allowing for more fine-grained analysis of the community's preference; however, further research is needed to assess whether this is actually a waste of human effort and a simple like button proves to be the most effective (Chamberlain et al., 2018).

In most crowdsourcing and citizen science systems users are rewarded for agreement and not punished for being disagreed with; however, other scoring models of this kind do exist (Rafelsberger and Scharl, 2009). It seems intuitive that positive behaviour be reinforced in crowdsourcing to encourage participation.

4.4. Limitations and Challenges

One drawback to offering unconstrained inputs is that users use them in different ways. There is a risk of accounts being used for malicious content, spreading advertising or for spamming. Users have different expectations that may lead to segregation into groups and data not being entered in a fashion that is expected. A significant challenge for unconstrained methods is the automatic processing of the threads (Maynard et al., 2012). There are a large quantity of unnecessary data associated with unconstrained inputs and removing this overhead is essential when processing on a large scale. The natural language processing needs to cope with ill-formed grammar and spelling, and sentences for which only context could make sense of the meaning. Additionally, the automatic processing of sentiment on poorly formed text is also challenging, with negative and compound assertions causing problems for automatic processing.

5. Conclusion

This paper explored how crowdsourcing and citizen science systems collect data and complete tasks, illustrated by a case study from the online language game-with-a-purpose *Phrase Detectives*. Understanding the interface design and task deconstruction are critical for enabling users to participate in such systems. Processing unconstrained input from users has applications within crowdsourcing and citizen science system design to allow users to express their solutions when they are beyond what the system was designed to collect. It would also enable efforts on a larger scale by analysing highly complex datasets created though social networking platforms.

6. Acknowledgements

The authors would like to thank all the players who played the game. The creation of the original game was funded by EPSRC project AnaWiki, EP/F00575X/1. The analysis of the data and preparation of this paper was funded by the DALI project, ERC Grant 695662

7. Bibliographical References

Agichtein, E., Castillo, C., Donato, D., Gionis, A., and Mishne, G. (2008). Finding high-quality content in social media. In *Proceedings of the 1st ACM International Conference on Web Search and Data Mining (WSDM'08)*, pages 183–194.

Aker, A., El-haj, M., Albakour, D., and Kruschwitz, U. (2012). Assessing crowdsourcing quality through objective tasks. In *Proceedings of the 8th International Conference on Language Resources and Evaluation (LREC'12)*.

Benkler, Y. and Nissenbaum, H. (2006). Commons-based peer production and virtue. *Journal of Political Philosophy*, 14(4):394–419.

Bunt, H., Alexandersson, J., Choe, J.-W., Fang, A. C., Hasida, K., Petukhova, V., Popescu-Belis, A., and Traum, D. (2012). ISO 24617-2: A semantically-based standard for dialogue annotation. In *Proceedings of the 8th International Conference on Language Resources and Evaluation (LREC'12)*, may.

Callison-Burch, C. and Dredze, M. (2010). Creating speech and language data with Amazon's Mechanical Turk. In *Proceedings of the 11th Annual Conference of the North American Chapter of the Association for Computational Linguistics (NAACL HLT 2010) Workshop on Creating Speech and Language Data with Amazon's Mechanical Turk (CSLDAMT '10)*.

Chamberlain, J. and O'Reilly, C. (2014). User performance indicators in task-based data collection systems. In *Proceedings of the 2014 iConference workshop MindTheGap'14*.

Chamberlain, J., Poesio, M., and Kruschwitz, U. (2008). Phrase Detectives: A web-based collaborative annotation game. In *Proceedings of the 2008 International Conference on Semantic Systems (I-Semantics'08)*.

Chamberlain, J., Poesio, M., and Kruschwitz, U. (2016). Phrase detectives corpus 1.0 crowdsourced anaphoric coreference. In *Proceedings of the 10th International Conference on Language Resources and Evaluation (LREC'16)*, may.

Chamberlain, J., Kruschwitz, U., and Poesio, M. (2018). Optimising crowdsourcing efficiency: Amplifying human computation with validation. *it - Information Technology*.

Chamberlain, J. (2014). Groupsourcing: Distributed problem solving using social networks. In *Proceedings of 2nd AAAI Conference on Human Computation and Crowdsourcing (HCOMP'14)*.

Clery, D. (2011). Galaxy evolution. Galaxy Zoo volunteers share pain and glory of research. *Science*, 333(6039):173–5.

Dabbish, L., Stuart, H. C., Tsay, J., and Herbsleb, J. D. (2014). Transparency and coordination in peer production. *Computing Research Repository (CoRR)*, abs/1407.0377.

Das, R. and Vukovic, M. (2011). Emerging theories and models of human computation systems: A brief survey. In *Proceedings of the 2nd International Workshop on Ubiquitous Crowdsouring (UbiCrowd'11)*, pages 1–4.

Elsholz, E., Chamberlain, J., and Kruschwitz, U. (2019). Exploring language style in chatbots to increase perceived product value and user engagement. In *Proceedings of the 2019 Conference on Human Information Interaction and Retrieval*, CHIIR '19, page 301–305, New York, NY, USA. Association for Computing Machinery.

Gillick, D. and Liu, Y. (2010). Non-expert evaluation of summarization systems is risky. In *Proceedings of the 11th Annual Conference of the North American Chapter of the Association for Computational Linguistics (NAACL HLT 2010) Workshop on Creating Speech and Language Data with Amazon's Mechanical Turk (CSLDAMT '10)*.

Gonella, P., Rivadavia, F., and Fleischmann, A. (2015). Drosera magnifica (Droseraceae): the largest New World sundew, discovered on Facebook. *Phytotaxa*, 220(3):257–267.

Hong, J. and Baker, C. F. (2011). How good is the crowd at "real" WSD? In *Proceedings of the 5th Linguistic Annotation Workshop (LAW V)*.

Howe, J. (2008). *Crowdsourcing: Why the power of the crowd is driving the future of business*. Crown Publishing Group.

Lakhani, K. R., Jeppesen, L. B., Lohse, P. A., and Panetta, J. A. (2007). The value of openness in scientific problem solving. Working Paper 07-050, Harvard Business School.

Malone, T., Laubacher, R., and Dellarocas, C. (2009). Harnessing crowds: Mapping the genome of collective intelligence. Research Paper No. 4732-09, Sloan School of Management, Massachusetts Institute of Technology, February.

Marge, M., Banerjee, S., and Rudnicky, A. I. (2010). Using the Amazon Mechanical Turk for transcription of spoken language. In *Proceedings of the 2010 IEEE International Conference on Acoustics Speech and Signal Processing (ICASSP'10)*.

Maynard, D., Bontcheva, K., and Rout, D. (2012). Challenges in developing opinion mining tools for social media. *Proceedings of the 8th International Conference on Language Resources and Evaluation (LREC'12) Workshop @NLP can u tag #user_generated_content.*

Novotney, S. and Callison-Burch, C. (2010). Cheap, fast and good enough: Automatic speech recognition with non-expert transcription. In *Proceedings of the 11th Annual Conference of the North American Chapter of the Association for Computational Linguistics (NAACL HLT 2010).*

Organisciak, P. and Twidale, M. (2015). Design facets of crowdsourcing. In *Proceedings of the 2015 iConference.*

Parameswaran, M. and Whinston, A. B. (2007). Social computing: An overview. *Communications of the Association for Information Systems*, 19.

Poesio, M., Chamberlain, J., Kruschwitz, U., Robaldo, L., and Ducceschi, L. (2013). Phrase Detectives: Utilizing collective intelligence for internet-scale language resource creation. *ACM Transactions on Interactive Intelligent Systems*, 3(1):1–44, April.

Poesio, M., Chamberlain, J., Paun, S., Yu, J., Uma, A., and Kruschwitz, U. (2019). A crowdsourced corpus of multiple judgments and disagreement on anaphoric interpretation. In *Proceedings of the 2019 Conference of the North American Chapter of the Association for Computational Linguistics: Human Language Technologies, Volume 1 (Long and Short Papers)*, pages 1778–1789, Minneapolis, Minnesota, June. Association for Computational Linguistics.

Quinn, A. J. and Bederson, B. B. (2011). Human computation: A survey and taxonomy of a growing field. In *Proceedings of the 2011 SIGCHI Conference on Human Factors in Computing Systems (CHI'11)*, pages 1403–1412.

Rafelsberger, W. and Scharl, A. (2009). Games with a purpose for social networking platforms. In *Proceedings of the 20th ACM Conference on Hypertext and Hypermedia.*

Raykar, V. C., Yu, S., Zhao, L. H., Valadez, G. H., Florin, C., Bogoni, L., and Moy, L. (2010). Learning from crowds. *Journal of Machine Learning Research*, 11:1297–1322.

Schenk, E. and Guittard, C. (2011). Towards a characterization of crowdsourcing practices. *Journal of Innovation Economics*, 7:93–107.

Sidlauskas, B., Bernard, C., Bloom, D., Bronaugh, W., Clementson, M., and Vari, R. P. (2011). Ichthyologists hooked on Facebook. *Science*, 332(6029):537.

Su, Q., Pavlov, D., Chow, J.-H., and Baker, W. C. (2007). Internet-scale collection of human-reviewed data. In *Proceedings of the 16th International Conference on World Wide Web (WWW'07)*, pages 231–240.

Tratz, S. and Hovy, E. (2010). A taxonomy, dataset, and classifier for automatic noun compound interpretation. In *Proceedings of the 48th Annual Meeting of the Association for Computational Linguistics (ACL'10).*

von Ahn, L. and Dabbish, L. (2008). Designing games with a purpose. *Communications of the ACM*, 51(8):58–67.

von Ahn, L. (2006). Games with a purpose. *Computer*, 39(6):92–94.

Wiggins, A. and Crowston, K. (2011). From conservation to crowdsourcing: A typology of citizen science. In *Proceedings of the 44th Hawaii International Conference on System Sciences (HICSS'11)*, pages 1–10.

Yang, H. and Lai, C. (2010). Motivations of Wikipedia content contributors. *Computers in Human Behavior*, 26.

Proceedings of the LREC 2020 Workshop "Citizen Linguistics in Language Resource Development", pages 35–39
Language Resources and Evaluation Conference (LREC 2020), Marseille, 11–16 May 2020

Leveraging Non-Specialists for Accurate and Time Efficient AMR Annotation

Mary Martin, Cecilia Mauceri, Martha Palmer and Christoffer Heckman
University of Colorado Boulder
Department of Computer Science, 430 UCB
Boulder, Colorado 80309-0430
<first>.<last>@colorado.edu

Abstract

Abstract Meaning Representations (AMRs), a syntax-free representation of phrase semantics (Banarescu et al., 2013), are useful for capturing the meaning of a phrase and reflecting the relationship between concepts that are referred to. However, annotating AMRs is time consuming and expensive. The existing annotation process requires expertly trained workers who have knowledge of an extensive set of guidelines for parsing phrases. In this paper, we propose a cost-saving two-step process for the creation of a corpus of AMR-phrase pairs for spatial referring expressions. The first step uses non-specialists to perform simple annotations that can be leveraged in the second step to accelerate the annotation performed by the experts. We hypothesize that our process will decrease the cost per annotation and improve consistency across annotators. Few corpora of spatial referring expressions exist and the resulting language resource will be valuable for referring expression comprehension and generation modeling.

Keywords: Abstract Meaning Representation, crowd-annotation, spatial referring expressions

The calendar is hanging below the cupboards.

```
(h / hang-01
  :arg0 () #agent, entity causing thing to be suspended
  :arg1 (c1 / calendar) #thing suspended
  :arg2 () #suspended from
  :location (b / below-01
    :op1 (c2 / cupboards))
```

The **flowers** in the middle of the **table**

```
(s / sit-01
  :arg1 (f / flowers) #thing sitting
  :arg2 (m / middle-01 #location or position
    :part-of (t / table))
```

Figure 1: Two referring expressions with their AMR parses. The color-coded bounding boxes and entity mentions indicate correspondences between the image and text.

1. Introduction

The relationship between the linguistic and visual representations of the same information is non-trivial. Not only is "a picture worth a thousand words", but there are also many possible ways to describe the same configuration of objects, i.e. the cupboard is *above* the sink or the sink is *below* the cupboard. Different syntax may also be used to communicate the same meaning. We need a linguistic representation where two expressions with the same underlying meaning have the same representation in order to build a correspondence between the text and image that can be used for visual question answering and referring expression comprehension and generation. AMRs (Abstract Meaning Representations) are one such representation.

Abstract Meaning Representations are a novel, natural language representation which is defined purely by the phrase's semantics. The novelty of this data structure lies in its ability to provide a single abstraction that can represent a number of different phrases. AMRs accomplish this through the use of relations and concepts that form a logical tree structure, as opposed to syntactic representations such as those produced through dependency and constituency parsing.

Using the AMR structure, we seek to annotate the object relationships from a corpora of spatial referring expressions. This representation effectively harnesses the spatial information in a given natural language sentence that is formulated based on a human's perception of the scene. AMR representations of spatial referring expressions will allow future research to explore how visual features relate to spatial relationships. Unfortunately, AMRs are expensive to annotate. There is no automated tool that has been deemed consistent enough to effectively create AMR parses of natural language sentences as there are with dependency and constituency parses. AMRs require annotators to derive the exact meaning of certain entities or "concepts" through context. This aspect, along with in-depth guidelines for structuring the trees, requires annotators to undergo extensive training.

Luckily, there are parts of the AMR annotation process that don't require expert knowledge. For example, it does not require training for humans to identify object relationships in phrases. Volunteers also do not require training in order to derive meaning from phrases and respond to queries such as "who is doing what to whom?" (Banarescu et al., 2013). We propose to divide the AMR annotation pipeline into two parts; the first part using crowd-workers and volunteer annotators, and the second, AMR experts. The intention of the tasks presented for non-specialist annotators is to create the closest possible result to an AMR without the need for domain specific knowledge. This approximate AMR can then be used as a starting point for expert annotation, limiting the role of experts to the more challenging annotation decisions. We hypothesize that this two step annotation will improve consistency and efficiency of annotation.

2. Related Work

2.1. Crowdsourcing Annotations

Crowdsourcing annotations is a common method for sourcing data for linguistics experiments and tasks. Techniques such as those used to annotate Question Answer (QA) Meaning Representations distribute the annotation process over multiple annotators in order to gain sufficient coverage when producing QA pairs (Michael et al., 2018). Methods for Semantic Role Labeling (SRL) in CROWD-IN-THE-LOOP improve upon previous practices for SRL by enabling annotators to produce gold-labeled training data without the need for expert involvement (Wang et al., 2017). We will take a similar approach to crowdsourcing in order to optimize the quality of data gathered by non-specialist volunteers, though we cannot eliminate the need for expert involvement. As opposed to splitting tasks for phrase coverage, we choose to split based on whether an annotation step requires expert knowledge.

2.2. Related Datasets

A few existing visual referring expressions datasets provide entity and relationship annotation. Flickr30k Entities includes annotations which link entity mentions and bounding boxes (Plummer et al., 2017). SentencesNYUv2 similarly aligns entity mentions and bounding boxes, and additionally provides adjective and preposition parsing (Kong et al., 2014). Visual Genome's region and scene graphs are most similar to AMRs (Krishna et al., 2017). Like AMRs, scene graphs are a formal representation of objects, relationships, and attributes. Like AMRs, they organize these elements in a graph structure and are syntax independent. In contrast to scene graphs, AMRs provide greater differentiation between roles than scene graphs do. To our knowledge, there is no dataset which pairs images and AMRs.

3. Proposed Method

Our goal is annotation, similar to that shown in Figure 1, consisting of referring expressions parsed into AMRs and linked to object bounding boxes. We source our referring expressions and bounding boxes from the SUN-Spot dataset (Mauceri et al., 2019). The challenge is to parse these referring expressions and link the entities to bounding boxes at low cost.

To complete this task, we propose an AMR annotation pipeline with three steps: (1) automated text preprocessing, (2) annotation by non-specialists, and (3) annotation by experts. With each step, the difficulty of the annotation tasks increase. We hypothesize that by ordering tasks in order of increasing difficulty, we can minimize the cognitive load of the annotators at each step, thus speeding annotation, decreasing overall cost, and improving consistency across annotators. The following sections detail each part of the pipeline.

3.1. Text Preprocessing

In order to structure the data for efficient annotation, we have implemented an automated text preprocessing function. This simple preprocessing step isolates certain parts of speech to assist with recognition of objects and spatial relationships. Automated preprocessing is done using the Stanford CoreNLP Toolkit (Manning et al., 2014) and Stanford Part-of-Speech (POS) Tagger (Toutanova et al., 2003). We intend to adopt some of the preprocessing techniques applied to phrases when generating the SentenceNYUv2 dataset (Kong et al., 2014). These techniques include using Stanford's coreference system to predict clusters of coreference mentions in order to identify pronouns. This can assist with identifying pronouns as they relate to objects in scenes (Clark and Manning, 2016).

The text preprocessing step also removes words from the phrase that are not relevant to the creation of an AMR. Such parts of speech include articles and conjunctions. In order for the phrase to be represented using a syntax-free graph, words in the sentence must pass through a lemmatizer. The lemmatizer reduces words to their root. This standardizes verb representation.

The preprocessing function also seeks to automate portions of the AMR annotation task which can produce inconsistent parses when manually performed by volunteers and workers. With the goal of consistency in mind, it is important to recognize where human error may occur in any process. We mitigate this by taking advantage of automated NLP tools that are accurate and easy to implement. The output of this function indicates important POS that highlight roles of words as they relate (or do not relate) to spatial relationships.

3.2. Annotation by Non-specialist Annotators

The next phase of annotation is performed by non-specialist annotators, such as crowd-workers and citizen scientist volunteers. Their job is twofold; the non-specialist annotators perform an initial pass identifying argument roles, and they label correspondences between object mentions in text and the location in the image.

In the final AMR annotation, words will be assigned to argument roles. However, argument roles are not familiar to most non-linguists. In order to provide a simplified annotation tool to non-specialist annotators, we chose a succinct set of familiar word classes that are analogous to argument roles. These classes include "subject", "relationship", "object" and "unrelated". Annotators are asked to classify all words in the processed phrase into one of these classes using a simple multiple choice interface. The proposed interface takes a similar form to that shown when decomposing QA-SRL questions into slot-based representations (FitzGerald et al., 2018). A mockup of our proposed inter-

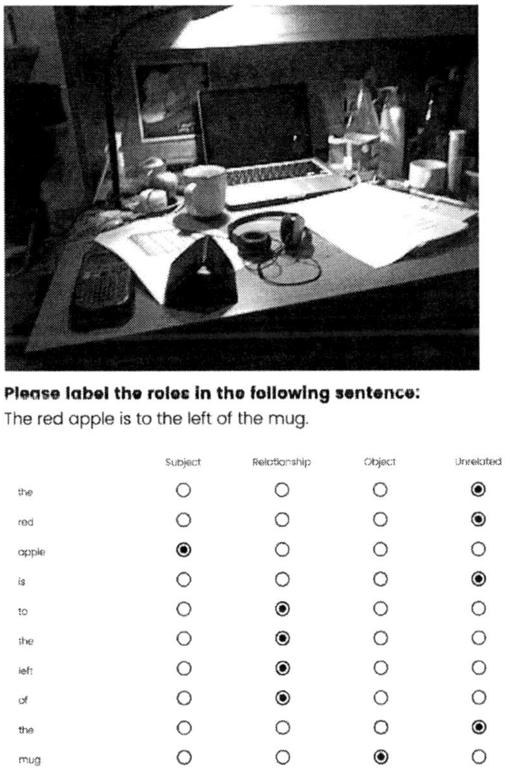

Figure 2: Example of annotation interface for approximate role labeling used by non-specialist annotators.

face is shown in Figure 2. We chose the word class role "relationship" in place of "preposition" in order to give annotators the choice to group chunks of words as a "relationship". During this annotation task, the annotators are provided with the full phrase, processed phrase and the original image for reference.

In the next annotation task, annotators label correspondences between the text and image. Our goal in annotating this dataset is to relate spatial relationships in images and referring expressions. Therefore, we wish to annotate any object mentions in the referring expression with links to the corresponding bounding box in the image. Highlighting the "subject" and "object" annotations from the previous step, we ask annotators to click on the corresponding object in the image. A similar task was successfully used to validate the referring expressions during the SUN-Spot dataset collection (Mauceri et al., 2019).

3.3. Annotation by Experts

The creation of AMRs from raw, unprocessed phrases is a time-consuming task because of the extensive set of guidelines that exist to create consistency between parses. To assist with this, experts will receive AMR proposals generated from the previous annotation steps instead of raw text. We hypothesize that approving, rejecting, and editing proposed AMRs is faster and easier than full annotation. The challenge is how to create appropriate proposals from the rough grained approximate roles provided by the non-specialist annotators.

Approximate Roles

```
Subject: apple
Relationship: to the left
Object: mug
```

Mapped to

```
(b / be-01
  arg1: (a / apple)
  arg2: (m / mug)
  location: (t / to the left)))
```

Corrected

```
(b / be-01
  arg1: (a / apple)
  arg2: (l / left
    op1: (m / mug)))
```

Figure 3: The approximate role labels are mapped to the AMR structure for review by experts. In this example, the subject and object roles are mapped to arg1 and arg2 and the relationship role is mapped to location. However, in the correct AMR, the relationship should be arg2. The expert must approve or reject the mapped AMRs. Rejected mapped AMRs are then hand-corrected.

In this generation process, the structure of spatial referring expressions comes to our assistance. Spatial referring expressions have two typical forms; either they contain a copula with a be-verb, or they use a position verb like "hang" or "sit". In both cases, the arg1 tends to be the subject of the referring expression, and the arg2 is either the location preposition or the object of the sentence. Using simple rules like these, we can establish a rule-based mapping for a large portion of our dataset. The expert annotator's role is to correct this mapping as shown in figure 3.

The data that the experts are presented with includes the full phrase, the processed phrase, the approximate argument role of each word, and the links between entities in the sentence and corresponding image. This data is meant to capture a simplified form of the relationship between the objects in the text and image domains. Through eliminating extraneous words and predetermining the roles of entities, we seek to introduce consistency and efficiency to this step in the pipeline. Consistency among a large number of examples is key in introducing a dataset that may act as ground truth when determining AMR parses of a variety of phrases.

An important aspect of this method is ensuring that the annotation pipeline provides improvements in consistency and efficiency as proposed. To assess the effectiveness of the process in these respects, we intend to compare the expense of annotating data from the perspective of the expert annotator. This involves evaluating the change in the time that it takes to complete one AMR, as well as qualitatively evaluating the change in the difficulty of the task based on feedback from the annotators. Ideally, an experiment such as this should yield results that indicate a significant decrease in annotation time, improvements in data quality, and a smoother process.

4. Future Work

4.1. Using Language Resources for Efficient Text Pre-processing

When designing tasks for annotation by non-specialists, phrase pre-processing has the potential to affect an annotator's interpretation of the phrase. For example, in a given word role classification task, identifying prepositions with multiple words may prove to be a challenge. Annotators must determine the words that define the spatial relationship between multiple objects. This presents a problem because interpretations of words that define relationships between objects may be inconsistent among annotators. A solution for this potential problem would be to present annotators with complete preposition phrases for role classification. In practice, this may involve chunking, for example "next to" instead of "next" and "to", in order to definitively demonstrate that the role of these words is a "relationship". Additionally, we intend to incorporate suggestions from expert annotators to develop ways to format the annotated phrases that will convert most directly to an AMR. In conjunction to taking an iterative approach for improving the data quality with expert feedback, we seek to improve the pipeline by automating much of the process if possible.

4.2. Using paired AMRs and RGB-D Images for Multi-modal Deep Learning

The graph structure of Abstract Meaning Representations makes them a suitable data structure for use with graph transformer networks, a variation of Graph Neural Networks (Scarselli et al., 2009). Graph Transformer Networks allow for the representation of heterogenous graph structures for machine learning tasks with graph structured input data (Yun et al., 2019). In this case, "heterogenous" refers to graphs with multiple edge types. The SUN-Spot dataset contains color images with an additional depth channel or RGB-D images. Through pairing AMRs and images where objects act as nodes on a graph and edges represent their spatial relationships, we hope to learn the relationship between the spatial relationships in phrases and depth images. Incorporating depth allows us to derive the locations of objects relative to others in the scene.

4.3. Automated AMR Parsing

Though the goal of annotating a referring expressions dataset is to capture spatial relationships in language, creating a large corpus of AMR-phrase pairs lends itself to other tasks. With an accumulation of phrases and corresponding ground truth AMR trees, this data would be well suited for a machine learning problem involving the automation of phrase parsing. A similar method has been used to automate Question Answer driven Semantic Role Labeling with successful results through a combination of phrase preprocessing and machine learning (FitzGerald et al., 2018).

5. Conclusion

We proposed an annotation pipeline with the goal of increasing efficiency in an expensive and time consuming process. By adopting and iteratively improving this method, our intention is to create a corpus that enables research involving solving problems in domains where AMRs have not previously been applied. In future work, we intend to demonstrate the benefits of linking this type of text abstraction to corresponding scenes. With this data, we will use deep neural networks to learn the connection between spatial relationships in natural language sentences using the RGB-D scenes that they are gathered from. Tangentially, we hope to move closer to a process for fully automated AMR parsing.

Acknowledgments

This work is partially supported by the National Science Foundation award number 1849357.

6. Bibliographical References

Banarescu, L., Bonial, C., Cai, S., Georgescu, M., Griffitt, K., Hermjakob, U., Knight, K., Koehn, P., Palmer, M., and Schneider, N. (2013). Abstract meaning representation for sembanking. In *Proceedings of the 7th linguistic annotation workshop and interoperability with discourse*, pages 178–186.

Clark, K. and Manning, C. D. (2016). Deep reinforcement learning for mention-ranking coreference models. In *Empirical Methods on Natural Language Processing*.

FitzGerald, N., Michael, J., He, L., and Zettlemoyer, L. (2018). Large-scale qa-srl parsing. In *Proceedings of the 56th Annual Meeting of the Association for Computational Linguistics (Volume 1: Long Papers)*, pages 2051–2060.

Kong, C., Lin, D., Bansal, M., Urtasun, R., and Fidler, S. (2014). What are you talking about? text-to-image coreference. In *CVPR*.

Krishna, R., Zhu, Y., Groth, O., Johnson, J., Hata, K., Kravitz, J., Chen, S., Kalantidis, Y., Li, L.-J., Shamma, D. A., et al. (2017). Visual genome: Connecting language and vision using crowdsourced dense image annotations. *International Journal of Computer Vision*, 123(1):32–73.

Manning, C., Surdeanu, M., Bauer, J., Finkel, J., Bethard, S., and McClosky, D. (2014). The Stanford CoreNLP natural language processing toolkit. In *Proceedings of 52nd Annual Meeting of the Association for Computational Linguistics: System Demonstrations*, pages 55–60, Baltimore, Maryland, June. Association for Computational Linguistics.

Michael, J., Stanovsky, G., He, L., Dagan, I., and Zettlemoyer, L. (2018). Crowdsourcing question-answer meaning representations. In *Proceedings of the 2018 Conference of the North American Chapter of the Association for Computational Linguistics: Human Language Technologies, Volume 2 (Short Papers)*, pages 560–568.

Plummer, B. A., Wang, L., Cervantes, C. M., Caicedo, J. C., Hockenmaier, J., and Lazebnik, S. (2017). Flickr30k entities: Collecting region-to-phrase correspondences for richer image-to-sentence models. *International Journal of Computer Vision*, 123(1):74–93.

Scarselli, F., Gori, M., Tsoi, A. C., Hagenbuchner, M., and Monfardini, G. (2009). The graph neural network model. *IEEE Transactions on Neural Networks*, 20(1):61–80, Jan.

Toutanova, K., Klein, D., Manning, C. D., and Singer, Y. (2003). Feature-rich part-of-speech tagging with a cyclic dependency network. In *Proceedings of the 2003 Conference of the North American Chapter of the Association for Computational Linguistics on Human Language Technology - Volume 1*, NAACL '03, page 173–180, USA. Association for Computational Linguistics.

Wang, C., Akbik, A., Chiticariu, L., Li, Y., Xia, F., and Xu, A. (2017). CROWD-IN-THE-LOOP: A hybrid approach for annotating semantic roles. In *Proceedings of the 2017 Conference on Empirical Methods in Natural Language Processing*, pages 1913–1922, Copenhagen, Denmark, September. Association for Computational Linguistics.

Yun, S., Jeong, M., Kim, R., Kang, J., and Kim, H. J. (2019). Graph transformer networks. In *Advances in Neural Information Processing Systems*, pages 11960–11970.

7. Language Resource References

Mauceri, C., Palmer, M., and Christoffer, H. (2019). SUN-Spot: An RGB-D Dataset With Spatial Referring Expressions. In *International Conference on Computer Vision Workshop on Closing the Loop Between Vision and Language*.

Proceedings of the LREC 2020 Workshop "Citizen Linguistics in Language Resource Development", pages 40–48
Language Resources and Evaluation Conference (LREC 2020), Marseille, 11–16 May 2020

The INCOMSLAV Platform: Experimental Website with Integrated Methods for Measuring Linguistic Distances and Asymmetries in Receptive Multilingualism

Irina Stenger, Klára Jágrová, Tania Avgustinova
Saarland University, Collaborative Research Center (SFB) 1102: Information Density and Linguistic Encoding,
Campus A 2.2, 66123 Saarbrücken, Germany
Project C4: INCOMSLAV – Mutual Intelligibility and Surprisal in Slavic Intercomprehension
ira.stenger@mx.uni-saarland.de, {kjagrova, avgustinova}@coli.uni-saarland.de

Abstract

We report on a web-based resource for conducting intercomprehension experiments with native speakers of Slavic languages and present our methods for measuring linguistic distances and asymmetries in receptive multilingualism. Through a website which serves as a platform for online testing, a large number of participants with different linguistic backgrounds can be targeted. A statistical language model is used to measure information density and to gauge how language users master various degrees of (un)intelligibilty. The key idea is that intercomprehension should be better when the model adapted for understanding the unknown language exhibits relatively low average distance and surprisal. All obtained intelligibility scores together with distance and asymmetry measures for the different language pairs and processing directions are made available as an integrated online resource in the form of a Slavic intercomprehension matrix (SlavMatrix).

Keywords: Slavic languages, intercomprehension, linguistic distance, asymmetric intelligibility, surprisal-based modelling

1. Introduction

1.1 Background

The terms "intercomprehension" (Doyé, 2005), "receptive multilingualism" (Braunmüller and Zeevaert, 2001) or "semi-communication" (Haugen, 1966) all refer, on the one hand, to a communicative practice of understanding an unknown foreign language based on already acquired linguistic repertoire, and on the other hand to a field of study which exploits linguistic similarities to model this special mode of language use. Its success relies on various types of information: linguistic, communicative, contextual, socio-demographic, etc. In the last decade, researchers focused mostly on uncovering the variables that influence intercomprehension between related languages (Gooskens and Swarte, 2017), with the assumption that the more linguistic similarities two languages share, the higher their degree of mutual intelligibility. This is quite apparent for modern Slavic languages as descendants of a single ancestor – Proto- or Common Slavic – that can be reconstructed by comparing diachronically and synchronically attested language varieties (Carlton, 1991; Comrie and Corbett, 1993). In general, linguistic phenomena may be unique to a language, shared between two languages, or common to many languages from a given family. In addition, Ringbom (2007: 11) distinguishes cross-linguistically between *objective similarities* (established as symmetrical) and *perceived similarities* (not necessarily symmetrical). Asymmetric intelligibility can be of linguistic nature, e.g., if language A has more complicated rules and/or irregular developments than language B, this results in structural asymmetry (Berruto, 2004). It can also be due to extra-linguistic and socio-demographic factors like attitude, language exposure, age, level of education, linguistic repertoire etc.

1.2 This Paper

In the INCOMSLAV project, we employ language modelling and information-theoretic concepts to investigate various intercomprehension scenarios with Slavic languages. We report on a website for conducting intercomprehension experiments as a resource. Besides the experiments, the site contains an integrated overview of the experimental results (intelligibility scores) together with the respective linguistic distances and surprisal as predictors for the intelligibility. We present our methods for measuring linguistic distances and asymmetries between related languages. A statistical model of linguistic distance and surprisal is used to measure information density and to gauge how language users master various degrees of distance and surprisal in view of partial incomprehensibility. The key idea here is that comprehension of an unknown but related language should be better, when the language model adapted for understanding the unknown language exhibits relatively low average distance and surprisal. Thus, our approach is based on three pillars: (i) linguistic resources, (ii) language technologies, (iii) experimental study of intercomprehension. This article is organized as follows. Section 2 gives an overview of the INCOMSLAV experiment platform and the conducted tests. Section 3 presents our methods for measuring linguistic distances and asymmetries among related languages. In Section 4 we analyze so far the obtained results that are made available in the Slavic intercomprehension matrix. Finally, some general conclusions are drawn and future work is outlined.

2. The INCOMSLAV platform

We test the mutual intelligibility of Slavic languages by means of the following tests: (i) intelligibility at the word level (individual words in spoken and written modality); (ii) intelligibility at the phrasal level (adjective-noun sequences in NPs); (iii) intelligibility at the sentence level (target words in predictive context). All experiments are available at http://intercomprehension.coli.uni-saarland.de with an interface in 11 Slavic languages, English and German. The participants have been recruited through universities, Prolific Academic, and social media. The respondents are continuously encouraged to participate in the challenges through the gamified character of the experiment website. They obtain a language medal for every completed experiment, can view their medal collection and select experiments with other languages to participate in. A short statistic overview of the automatically classified correct answers together with the average response time is displayed at the end of each experiment. The participants have the opportunity to see their performance in different challenges in a visualization of their achievements on a timeline showing the individual completed experiments. They get an immediate feedback in which unknown but related language they have achieved better results. These intercomprehension scores reveal what is known as *inherent* intelligibility, i.e. based on structural linguistic similarities (Gooskens, 2019). What's more, our website can be used as an e-learning component of intercomprehension courses on Slavic languages offered at universities or elsewhere. To this effect, we provide an additional try-again functionality for already completed experiments. Thus, the students have the opportunity to repeat completed tasks once again towards the end of a course and to compare the initial results (inherent intelligibility) with the intercomprehension scores achieved after a focused teaching intervention, with the latter results revealing the so-called *acquired* intelligibility. An acquired *lingua receptiva* can apply to less related or unrelated languages, too (Muikku-Werner, 2014). And *mediated* receptive multilingualism (Branets et al., 2019) utilizing a bridge language can ease the understanding even between typologically distant languages, for example, when German participants with some training in Russian (RU) try to understand Bulgarian (BG) through RU in our experiments. In the following sections, we present only results of the inherent intelligibility for Slavic native speakers in an intercomprehension scenario. With regard to socio-demographic data, the participants are asked to specify their age, sex, level of education, linguistic repertoire, learning duration, assumed proficiency of (non)-native languages in written and spoken modality, place/country of residence, linguistic surroundings, etc. This information can be used for further analyses concerning the influence of extra-linguistic and socio-demographic factors on receptive multilingualism. After having completed the registration process, including the questionnaire, the participants are introduced to the challenge.

2.1 Intelligibility at the word level

This challenge is designed as a cognate guessing task. The participants are asked to translate randomized written and spoken stimuli into their native language. In the written condition, participants see the stimuli on their screen, one by one, and have 10 seconds to translate each stimulus. In the spoken condition, participants listen to the stimuli one by one with the task to provide a written translation within the same duration (10 seconds). In the spoken translation task, each word is played twice. The time limit is chosen based on the experience from other intercomprehension experiments, including, among others, a pilot study by Golubović (2016). The allocated time is supposed to be sufficient for typing even the longest words, but not long enough for using a dictionary or an online translation tool. It is possible to finish before the 10 seconds are over by either clicking on the 'Next' button or pressing 'Enter' on the keyboard. After 10 seconds, the participants hear or see the next stimulus on their screen. The order of stimuli presentation is randomized. The system saves everything that is entered, regardless of whether a participant confirms the translation by pressing the return key (or clicking 'Next') or not. The results are automatically categorized as 'correct' or 'wrong' via pattern matching with predefined correct answers and acceptable alternatives. An immediate feedback is given in the shape of an emoticon on the left at the bottom of the page – a thumb up for a successful translation or a sad face for a wrong or missing translation. There is a tolerance for lower/upper case and diacritical signs, i.e. if translations were entered without diacritics, but are otherwise correct, the participants get a positive feedback. The responses can then be checked manually for typographical errors in the final analysis.

2.2 Intelligibility at the phrasal level

This challenge is designed as a translation of noun and adjective sequences, with the adjective occurring pre- or post-nominally. For each stimulus phrase, the participants have 20 seconds for entering a translation into their language. The individual target words, together with the words directly preceding them, are extracted from the sentence stimuli in order to be also tested in their base forms (if applicable) at the word level.

2.3 Intelligibility at the sentence level

This challenge is designed as a cloze (fill-in-the-gap) translation task. The respondents see initially only the first word of the sentence. They are prompted to click on the word so that the next word in the sentence appears. After they have clicked through and consequently read the entire stimulus sentence in that way, a box appears at the position of the last word, which should be translated. This method ensures that participants read each sentence word by word. There are two separate time limits: one for clicking and reading through the sentence and one for entering the translation of the target word. The latter is automatically set by the system to 20-30 seconds, depending on the length of the sentence. The time limit for clicking and reading through the whole sentence is set to a maximum value of 300 seconds.

3. Methods for measuring intelligibility

In the INCOMSLAV framework, we developed measuring methods of immediate relevance to the concept of receptive multilingualism. Similarities between Slavic orthographies were captured by (modifications of) the Levenshtein metric (Levenshtein, 1966). Being frequently used as a predictor of phonetic and orthographic similarity (Beijering, Gooskens, and Heeringa, 2008; Gooskens, 2007; Vanhove, 2014), this mathematical distance is, however, completely symmetric. In order to account for the asymmetries of intercomprehension, additional measures of conditional entropy and surprisal (Shannon, 1948) were applied. Conditional character adaptation entropy and word adaptation surprisal (Mosbach et al., 2019; Stenger, 2019; Stenger et al., 2017) quantify the difficulties humans encounter when mapping one orthographic system on another and reveal the asymmetries in language pairs. Consider, for example, the language pairs Czech (CS) - Polish (PL) (West Slavic with Latin script) and BG-RU (South and East Slavic with Cyrillic script). While having similar lexical distances (share of non-cognates) of 10-15% depending on the direction, CS and PL are orthographically more distant from each other than BG and RU (for more details see Jágrová et al., 2017).

Our measures suggest that Czech readers should have more difficulties reading PL than vice versa, and that the asymmetry between BG and RU is very small with a minimal predicted advantage for Russian readers (Stenger et al., 2017). Furthermore, the word-length normalized adaptation surprisal appears to be a better predictor than the aggregated Levenshtein distance when the same stimuli sets in different language pairs are compared (Stenger, Avgustinova, and Marti, 2017). Previous research shows that additional factors such as word length, neighborhood density and word frequency play a significant role in spoken word recognition without context (Kürschner, van Bezooijen, and Gooskens, 2008). We also found (Stenger, 2019) that word length as an explanatory variable is essential in the recognition of written South Slavic (BG, Macedonian (MK), and Serbian (SR)) stimuli by Russian readers, since the South Slavic words are generally shorter than their RU and East Slavic (Ukrainian (UK) and Belarusian (BE)) cognates. Neighbors are linguistically defined as word forms that are very similar to the stimulus word and may therefore serve as competing responses (ibid.), for example the BG word *цел* (*cel*) 'target' with the correct RU translation *цель* (*cel'*) has two RU neighbors: *мел* (*mel*) 'chalk' and *цех* (*cech*) 'workshop', while the BG word *автомобил* (*avtomobil*) 'car' has no neighbors. BG and SR written intelligibility to Russian native speakers shows that the higher the neighborhood density, the lower is the number of successful translations, although this is not the case for UK, BE, and MK stimuli when presented to Russian readers. According to our experimental results, the frequency of cognates is not a reliable predictor for Russian readers. In reality, the orthographic and phonetic correspondences (their nature, position, and frequency) can considerably influence intercomprehension. Investigating Cyrillic script intelligibility to Russian readers, we saw that (i) identical orthographic correspondences increase intelligibility, while non-identical correspondences yield a barrier, and (ii) cognates are generally easier to understand if the beginning of the word is identical (ibid.). Until recently, the role of context in intercomprehension has been addressed in relatively few studies. In a monolingual situation, statistical language models (LMs) provide information about the predictability of words in context. Levy (2008) showed that n-gram LMs, specifically trigrams, performed well at predicting the processing effort measured by the reading times of variably difficult texts. In information theory, a commonly used unpredictability measure is surprisal. It can be thought of as a measure for the information conveyed by a linguistic unit and scales the cognitive effort required to process this information (Crocker, Demberg, and Teich 2016). The lower the surprisal, the more predictable a word is in a sentence, given its preceding words. Whenever there is a drop in surprisal after a word, the word with the lower surprisal should be highly predictable after its preceding word. We investigated the intelligibility of highly predictable target words in PL sentences presented to Czech readers (Jágrová et al., 2018), and saw that predictions based on surprisal scores do not always agree with the actually observed intercomprehension difficulty by humans. In order to study the role of predictive context and its correlation with intelligibility in the intercomprehension scenario quantitatively, we presented 149 PL target words both in highly predictive sentential context (cloze probability ≥90%, Block and Baldwin, 2010) and without context to Czech readers (Jágrová and Avgustinova, 2019). We found that surprisal had a significant correlation with target words that were non-cognates or false friends (there were 65.1% cognates, 11.4% non-cognates, and 23.5% false friends). During the disambiguation of these, readers did rely on context rather than on word similarity (ibid.).

4. Intercomprehension resources

Currently, we provide 162 online experiments (spoken and written individual word translation (40-60 words per spoken and written challenge), phrasal translation (30-35 phrases per challenge), and word translation in predictive context (10-20 sentences per challenge) for native speakers of 11 Slavic languages (BE, BG, CS, Croatian (HR), MK, PL, RU, SR, Slovak (SK), Slovenian, UK) as well as German and English. The designed experimental sets stem from a collection of parallel lists of internationalisms, Panslavic vocabulary, cognates from Swadesh lists[1], frequency lists of the respective languages (e.g. Křen (2010) for CS, Ljaševskaja and Šarov (2009) for RU) and resources from available corpora (InterCorp, Czech National Corpus, Russian National Corpus etc.).

About 2000 native speakers[2] participated in the challenges. The online available Slavic intercomprehension matrix (SlavMatrix)[3] contains currently obtained intelligibility scores and measures of linguistic distances and asymmetries for different language pairs and processing directions. Table 1 gives a high-level overview of the SlavMatrix.

Level	Sublevel
Intelligibility	Individual words: Automatic Panslavic vocabulary Top 100 Verbs
	Phrases (adjective-noun combinations)
	Words in predictive contexts
Predictors	Linguistic distances: Orthographic Lexical Phonetic Morphological Syntactic
	Conditional entropy
	Word adaptation surprisal (WAS)
Correlations	Intelligibility with Levenshtein distance
	Intelligibility with lexical distance
	Intelligibility with conditional entropy
	Intelligibility with word adaptation surprisal

Table 1: High-level overview of the SlavMatrix.

[1] Refer to Angelov (2004), Likomanova (2004), and Swadesh lists for Slavic languages, accessed on 2015-04-22.

[2] Status of 2020-03-02.

[3] http://intercomprehension.coli.uni-saarland.de/en/SlavMatrix/Results/

In Section 4.1 we discuss the level of intelligibility of individual words, in Section 4.2 we analyze the level of predictors, and in Section 4.3 we address the level of correlations.

4.1 SlavMatrix: individual words

The sublevel of individual words contains the following data: (i) automatically calculated experimental results, (ii) experimental results for the Panslavic vocabulary, (iii) experimental results for the 100 most frequent nouns (Top 100), and (iv) experimental results for verbs. The automatically calculated results cover all individual word translation tasks. Since reading and listening are different cognitive activities, we differentiate between the written and the spoken version of the tests and consider in the following the reading intelligibility only. Intelligibility scores are calculated for each of the above mentioned sublevels. The scores are converted to percentages by dividing the number of correct responses by the number of items in the test (and multiplying the result by 100). According to the automatically calculated experimental results, the highest scores were observed for Slovak participants reading CS (84.1%[4]), and for Croatian subjects reading SK (84.0%). As expected, Czech readers also understand SK at a high level (77.8%). Slovak readers understand HR at 68.0%. Here we have an asymmetry of 16.0% in favor of Croatian readers. The smallest intelligibility scores were observed for Slovak subjects reading UK (4.0%). This can be explained by the fact that SK is written with the Latin script and UK with the Cyrillic script. Thus, UK can generally only be understood by readers who know the Cyrillic script. Across the West Slavic languages with Latin script (PL, CS, and SK) and East Slavic languages with the Cyrillic script (BE, RU, and UK) the comprehensibility values are at a high level in both sub-groups, e.g. participants of East Slavic languages managed to translate more than 74% of the words correctly and readers of West Slavic languages reached almost 68%. All these percentages are intelligibility scores based on answers that were automatically classified as correct by the website.

For more precise and representative data, we have considered the sublevel of experimental results for Panslavic vocabulary that has been checked manually in the final analysis. The stimuli are cognates (etymologically related words) containing historical cross-lingual orthographic correspondences, e.g. BG–RU: *б:бл*, *ж:жд*, *ла:оло*, *я:е* etc. (for more details see Fischer et al., 2015; Fischer et al. 2016). The initial hypothesis was that correct cognate recognition would be the key to successful intercomprehension. The experimental results show in particular that among the East Slavic languages UK is more understandable to Russian readers than BE. The average comprehensibility values for UK and BE stimuli are relatively high – almost 86% and 73% respectively. Among the three South Slavic languages, BG is the most understandable one for Russian readers, with an average comprehensibility value of approx. 71%, followed by MK with 62% and SR with almost 59%. Thus, we can state for Russian readers[5] that, on average, a successful cross-lingual recognition of individual East and South Slavic cognates is generally registered here. Concerning the language pair BG and RU, the results show that there is virtually no asymmetry in written intelligibility between these languages: the Bulgarian participants understand a slightly larger number of the 120 RU words (74.67%) than the Russian participants understand the 120 BG words they are presented with (71.33%)[6]. This can be explained by the fact that there are only slight differences between the two languages on the graphic-orthographical level (for more details see Stenger et al., 2017).

4.2 SlavMatrix: predictors

Two measurement methods provide predictions of mutual intelligibility between (closely) related languages: Levenshtein distance (LD, here as orthographic string edit distance) and word adaptation surprisal (WAS) (see Table 1). LD is, in its basic implementation, a symmetric similarity measure between two strings, in our case between written words. It quantifies the number of operations in order to transform one word into another. When computing LD for a pair of words, three different character transformations are considered: deletion, insertion, and substitution. These operations are assigned weights. In the simplest form of the algorithm, all operations have the same cost. We use 0 for the cost of mapping a character to itself, e.g. *a:a*, and a cost of 1 to align it to a character of the same kind (vowel characters vs. consonant characters), e.g. *a:o*. All vowel-to-consonant combinations are given a weight of 4.5 (most expensive) in the algorithm. Thus, we obtain distances which are based on linguistically motivated alignments. In more sensitive versions, a base and a diacritic may be distinguished. For example, the base of *ë* is *e*, and the diacritic is the diaeresis. Even though it is not exactly clear what weight should be attributed to each of the components, it is generally assumed that differences in the base will usually confuse the reader to a much greater extent than diacritical differences. If two characters have the same base but differ in diacritics, we assign them a substitution cost of 0.5 (for more details s. Mosbach et al., 2019). In our analysis we consider normalized LD (nLD) in accordance with the assumption that a segmental difference in a word of, e.g., two segments has a stronger impact on intelligibility than a segmental difference in a word of, e.g. ten segments (Beijering, Gooskens, and Heeringa, 2008). The nLD of BG–RU: *език–язык* (*ezik–jazyk*) 'tongue/language' is 2/4=0.5 or 50%. Measuring the orthographic distance on the basis of the Levenshtein

[4] This value cannot be compared to the intelligibility scores for cognate lists in the other language pairs, since the stimuli sets for CS-SK included non-cognates. The intelligibility score for CS-SK cognates might in fact be higher.

[5] 119 Russian native speakers took part in the experiments with 340 East and South Slavic stimuli, the mean age of the participants was 34 years, ¾ women and ¼ men. We only analyzed answers from participants who indicated that they did not know the stimulus language and only of the initial challenge for each participant in order to avoid any learning effects (for more details see Stenger, 2019).

[6] The analysis of the collected material is based on the answers of 37 native speakers of BG (31 women and 6 men, mean age 27 years) and 40 native speakers of RU (32 women and 8 men, mean age 33 years) of the initial challenge. All participants have indicated that they did not know the stimulus language (for more details see Mosbach et al., 2019).

algorithm allows us to model the mutual intelligibility based on the following hypothesis: The larger the distance, the more difficult it is to comprehend an unknown language. Displaying a more generalized view of modelling mutual intelligibility among Slavic languages, the nLD matrix (Table 2) shows aggregated orthographic distances (in percentages) between East and South Slavic languages on 190 cognate pairs of Common Slavic vocabulary, published in (Carlton, 1991) (for more details on the used material see Stenger, 2019).

stimulus language	native language					
	BE	BG	MK	RU	SR	UK
BE	0	40.66	41.11	27.23	41.98	36.56
BG	40.66	0	17.04	32.05	24.89	35.52
MK	41.11	17.04	0	32.19	19.37	36.37
RU	27.23	32.05	32.19	0	32.09	22.77
SR	41.98	24.89	19.37	32.09	0	33.03
UK	36.56	35.52	36.37	22.77	33.03	0

Table 2: Aggregated nLD as predictor of mutual intelligibility among BE, BG, MK, RU, SR, and UK.

In general, the average symmetrical Levenshtein distance values of the 15 analyzed East and South Slavic language pairs are below 42%, which indicates a relatively high orthographic similarity between these languages (all using Cyrillic) and, hence, mutual intelligibility on the orthographic level. According to the nLD matrix, mean normalized orthographic distances between South Slavic languages are smaller than between East Slavic languages, which leads to the assumption that readers of a South Slavic language may be better able to understand cognates in written texts of in another South Slavic language than East Slavic readers who are confronted with a written text in another East Slavic language. Furthermore BG and MK are the closest language pair in the South Slavic subgroup, since they get the smallest symmetric orthographic distance (17.04%). As already pointed out, a disadvantage of this string-edit method is that the LD cannot show any asymmetries depending on the processing direction in a given language pair. Given two aligned words, we can also compute for them the word adaptation surprisal (WAS), which, intuitively, measures how confused a reader would be trying to map a character of the stimulus word to a character of the target word. In order to define WAS we introduce the notation of character adaptation surprisal (CAS) which is defined as follows:

$$\mathrm{CAS}(L1 = c1|L2 = c2) = -\log_2 P(L1 = c1|L2 = c2)$$

$L1$ – native language, c1 – character of $L1$

$L2$ – stimulus language, c2 – character of $L2$

Now, WAS between two words is computed by summing up the CAS values of the contained characters in the aligned word pair (for more details see Mosbach et al., 2019; Stenger 2019). Note that in contrast to LD, CAS and WAS are not symmetric. Moreover, the WAS highly depends on the number of available word pairs. Computing CAS (and therefore also WAS) depends on the conditional probability *P*, which is based on corpus statistics of the aligned word pairs by means of the Levenshtein algorithm. For example, the RU character *а* (which occurs 175 times) corresponds exclusively to the BG character *а* (which occurs 194 times). The BG character *а* may correspond to the RU character *а* (175 times), *о* (15 times) or *я* (4 times) (these examples are based on the 291 cognate pairs, for more details see Stenger et al., 2020). Thus, for our example above, we would get $P(\text{BG} = \text{а} \mid \text{RU} = \text{а}) = 175/175 = 1.0$, while $P(\text{RU}=\text{а} \mid \text{BG} = \text{а}) = 175/194 \approx 0.9$, $P(\text{RU} = \text{о} \mid \text{BG} = \text{а}) = 15/194 \approx 0.07$, and $P(\text{RU} = \text{я} \mid \text{BG} = \text{а}) = 4/194 \approx 0.02$. In such a case, we can expect a Russian reader to have more difficulties to correctly guess which characters in RU correspond to the BG one he/she is confronted with. As in the case with the LD, we normalized the WAS and calculated the average value of the normalized WAS (nWAS) for 190 cognate pairs of the Common Slavic vocabulary (Carlton, 1991). The nWAS matrix (Table 3) displays the mean nWAS (in bits) between selected languages reflecting the asymmetry and complexity of the mapping of one orthographic system on another, based on the following assumption: The higher the mean nWAS, the more difficult it is to comprehend the unknown language. According to the nWAS matrix, BG and MK are not only the closest language pair in the South Slavic sub-group, but there is an orthographic asymmetry between BG and MK in favor of MK. The mean nWAS gives us the following values: 0.66 bits for Bulgarian readers of MK and 0.49 bits for Macedonian readers of BG, thus predicting that a Bulgarian reader may have more difficulties reading MK than vice versa.

stimulus language	native language					
	BE	BG	MK	RU	SR	UK
BE	0	1.18	1.12	0.69	1.09	0.80
BG	1.39	0	0.49	1.18	0.82	1.36
MK	1.50	0.64	0	1.28	0.82	1.46
RU	0.72	0.98	0.90	0	0.87	0.68
SR	1.36	0.87	0.72	1.13	0	1.23
UK	0.79	1.16	1.09	0.66	0.99	0

Table 3: Mean nWAS as predictor of mutual intelligibility among BE, BG, MK, RU, SR, and UK.

4.3 SlavMatrix: correlations

Normalized LDs were calculated for all word pairs of the respective experimental tasks in order to correlate the orthographic distance with the human intelligibility scores. For example, in the Cyrillic script intelligibility tests for Russian native speakers, mentioned in Section 4.1, the negative correlations were statistically significant for all analyzed language pairs: BE–RU ($r = -0.509$, $p = 3.17e\text{-}05$), BG–RU ($r = -0.566$, $p = 1.47e\text{-}11$), MK–RU ($r = -0.305$, $p < 0.05$), SR–RU ($r = -0.659$, $p = 1.87e\text{-}07$), UK–RU ($r = -0.456$, $p < 0.0005$), although they could be classified as low to medium. The highest negative correlation is characteristic for the SR–RU language pair. In other words, the initial hypothesis that small orthographic distances between two cognates correlate with high intelligibility values – and large orthographic distances with low intelligibility values – can be considered confirmed. In addition, we also calculated the nWAS for each cognate pair of the above mentioned tests. The significant negative correlation was recorded only for the UK–RU language pair ($r = -0.491$, $p = 6.67e\text{-}05$), suggesting that the complexity of a mapping between two cognates measured by the nWAS method plays the most important role in the recognition of individual cognates for the UK–RU language pair.

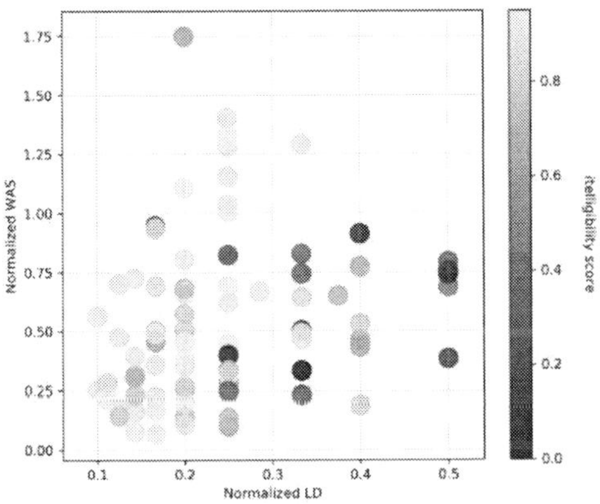

Figure 1: Intelligibility score depending on normalized LD and normalized WAS, BG for Russian readers

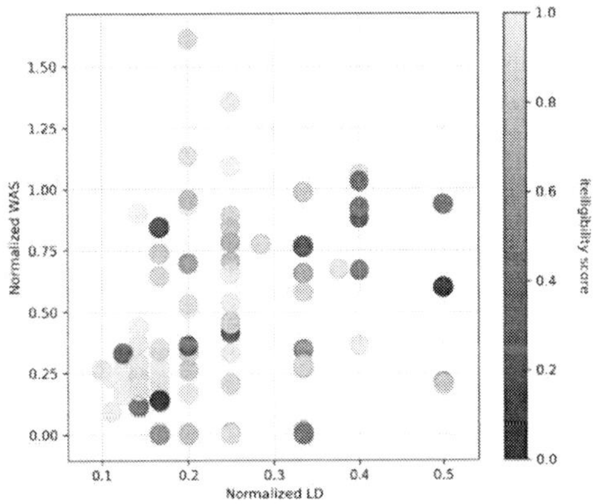

Figure 2: Intelligibility score depending on normalized LD and normalized WAS, RU for Bulgarian readers

For the other three language pairs the negative correlations were not significant: BG–RU (r = –0.135, p = 0.142), MK–RU (r = –0.131, p = 0.364), and SR–RU (r = –0.270, p = 0.058). For the fifth language pair BE–RU, the calculated correlation was even slightly positive (r = 0.196, not significant p = 0.134), which speaks against the initial hypothesis (for more details see Stenger, 2019). The question is why the correlation at the cognate level is so low and insignificant for three language pairs (with the BE–RU language pair representing an outlier with regard to the formulated hypothesis). Intuitively, it seems plausible that a stimulus word is easier to understand if it is more similar to a cognate in the target language. So, a possible explanation could be that identical characters can have a CAS value on the basis of the nWAS method, which automatically increases the total nWAS value. A modified nWAS method (described in Mosbach et al., 2019 and in Stenger, 2019) allows us to consider CAS values for all identical characters with costs of 0 in a manual post-processing step. After the modification of the nWAS method, a negative correlation between the modified nWAS and the test results was found for all language pairs: BE–RU (r = –0.035), BG–RU (r = –0.210), MK–RU (r = –0.155), SR–RU (r = –0.396), UK–RU (r = –0.555). However, the examination of the statistical results for their significance showed that the negative correlations were only for three language pairs at a significant level: BG–RU ($p < 0.05$), SR–RU ($p < 0.005$), and UK–RU (p = 4.156e-06) (for more details see Stenger, 2019). As already mentioned in Section 1.2, the intercomprehension should be better, when the language model adapted for understanding the unknown language exhibits relatively low average distance and surprisal. Concerning the mutual intelligibility between BG and RU (described in Section 4.1) the nLD and nWAS account for 32% (R^2 = 0.32) of the variance in the intelligibility scores for Russian readers and for only 14% (R^2 = 0.14) of the variance in the intelligibility scores for Bulgarian readers, which leaves the majority of variance unexplained (see Figures 1 and 2). Note that the calculated mean nLD and nWAS data are based here on a small experimental corpus. There are a number of arguments why distance measurements should be calculated not on the basis of the experimental material, but on the basis of larger amounts of data. In particular, distance measurements become more stable and correlate better with mutual intelligibility when calculated on larger data (van Heuven, Gooskens, and van Bezooijen, 2015). This relationship may be different if the distance measurements are specifically based on the experimental material used in the intelligibility test (ibid.). The CAS values are different and depend on the respective cognate lists. If the scope of the cognate list is extended with further pairs, the CAS values may change, which would lead to a change in the nWAS values, too. In the web-based experiments, subjects are confronted with a limited amount of data. Therefore, the regularity of one or the other correspondence from the cognate lists of the experimental material does not necessarily correspond to the one observed in the respective correspondences from a larger corpus. We measured nLD and nWAS values on the experimental material and correlated them with the intelligibility values from the web-based experiments, namely, the intelligibility scores based on the initial challenge for each participant in order to avoid any learning effects (see Section 4.1). The WAS values between language A and language B are not necessarily the same as between language B and language A, which indicates an advantage of the surprisal-based method compared to LD in modelling asymmetry. We calculated the mean nWAS for BG and RU using a cognate word list from the intelligibility tests (see Section 4.1). For the BG–RU language pair the difference in the mean nWAS is very small: 0.46 bits for the RU to BG transformation and 0.50 bits for the BG to RU transformation, with a very small amount of asymmetry of 0.04 bits. These results predict that speakers of RU reading BG words are more uncertain than speakers of BG reading RU words. This is in accordance with the experimental results where the language combination with the slightly higher mean nWAS (speakers of RU reading BG words) had a slightly lower intelligibility score (see Section 4.1).

5. Discussion and Future Work

In this paper we presented the INCOMSLAV platform as a web-based resource for conducting intercomprehension experiments with native speakers of Slavic languages, and illustrated our methods for measuring linguistic distances and asymmetries in receptive multilingualism. All obtained intelligibility scores as well as distance and asymmetry measures are made available as an integrated online resource in the form of a Slavic intercomprehension matrix (SlavMatrix), which will be maintained and further completed as new data and correlations become available.

Among presented intelligibility tests we discussed here automatically calculated experimental results of individual words as well as manually checked experimental results for a Panslavic vocabulary. Even though it may seem artificial to test individual words without context, since the latter may provide helpful information, our underlying assumption is that the cognate recognition is a precondition of success in reading intercomprehension. If the reader correctly recognizes a minimal proportion of words, he or she will be able to piece the written message together. An important practical criterion for choosing a test is the ease with which it can be developed, administered and analyzed. If more languages should be tested, extensive time and effort would be needed to collect a large number of participants. Since we have the most completed experiments in different language combinations for the word level, we decided to focus here on the individual word translation tasks. We need to collect and further analyze the experimental results at the phrasal and sentence levels, too. Recently, the INCOMSLAV platform also provides the LADO experiments (Language Analysis for Determination of Origin) and collects experimental data evaluating in fact the listening interpretation ability of the participants not only in foreign languages, but also in their own language, for example, recognition of RU segments (LADO 1) and prosody (LADO 2) among Russian native speakers.

Related research has already shown that *inherent* intelligibility can be predicted quite well by linguistic distance and that a short word list provides sufficient input for computing the distance measures needed (Gooskens and van Heuven, 2019). Therefore it may be an option to rely on distance measurements rather than on costly functional testing in order to investigate how well speakers of closely related languages will be able to understand each other (ibid). We presented two measurements of linguistic distance and asymmetry as potential predictors of mutual intelligibility between (closely) related languages: normalized Levenshtein distance (nLD) as orthographic distance and normalized word adaptation surprisal (nWAS) as orthographic asymmetry between Slavic languages. As already discussed in Section 3, the mean nWAS at the language level appears to be a better predictor than the aggregated nLD when the same stimuli sets in different language pairs are compared (Stenger, Avgustinova, and Marti, 2017). In this contribution we were also able to show that the mean nWAS can be a reliable measure when explaining small asymmetries in intelligibility between BG and RU (see Section 4.3). However, at the cognate level, the nLD correlates better with the experimental results as nWAS. As other inter-comprehension research shows, each pair of cognates has its own constellation of factors that influence intelligibility, whereby one factor can overlay another (Kürschner, van Bezooijen, and Gooskens, 2008). In addition, factors and corresponding models are language-dependent, as each language combination poses different challenges to the readers. In summary, this means that each model has its limits and there is room for improvement by taking into account the influence of additional factors, for example, neighborhood density (the number of word forms that are similar to the stimulus word), the effects of character context, within-word position, consonants vs. vowels, dialects or archaic terms etc.

Our resources, including *incom.py*[7] – a toolbox for calculating linguistic distances and asymmetries between related languages, can be of interest to other researchers working on intercomprehension and to teachers of multilingual language courses. In the next phase, we plan to extend the *SlavMatrix* resources by an *IncomSlavCorpus*, providing researches of receptive multilingualism with the experimental material used in our tests and with all correlated intercomprehension results. In addition to structural characteristics of the languages a broader approach will include extra-linguistic factors (e.g. language exposure) and individual factors (e.g. age, linguistic repertoire, language learning experience, education level) that contribute to understanding unknown but related languages.

6. Acknowledgements

We wish to thank Hasan Alam for his support in the implementation of the SlavMatrix. This work has been funded by the Deutsche Forschungsgemeinschaft (DFG, German Research Foundation) – Project-ID 232722074 – SFB 1102.

7. Bibliographical References

Angelov, A. (2004). EuroComSlav Basiskurs – der panslavische Wortschatz. http://www.eurocomslav.de/BIN/inhalt.htm, accessed 2016-02-17.

Beijering, K., Gooskens, C. and Heeringa, W. (2008). Predicting intelligibility and perceived linguistic distance by means of the Levenshtein algorithm. In M. van Koppen & B. Botma (Eds.), *Linguistics in the Netherlands* 2008. John Benjamins, Amsterdam pp. 13–24.

Berruto, G. (2004). Sprachvarietät – Sprache (Gesamtsprache, historische Sprache). In U. Ammon et al. (Eds.), *Soziolinguistik. Ein internationales Handbuch zur Wissenschaft von Sprache und Gesellschaft*, 1. Teilband. Walter de Gruyter, Berlin, New York, pp. 188–195.

Branets, A., Bahtina, D., and Anna Verschik. (2019). Mediated receptive multilingualism: Estonian-Russian-Ukrainian case study. *Linguistic Approaches to Bilingualism*: 1–32.

Braunmüller, K. and Zeevaert, L. (2001). Semikommunikation, rezeptive Mehrsprachigkeit und verwandte Phänomene. Eine bibliographische Bestandsaufnahme, Arbeiten zur Mehrsprachigkeit, Folge B, 19, Universität Hamburg, Hamburg.

Block, C. K. and Baldwin, C. L. (2010). Cloze probability and completion norms for 498 sentences: Behavioral and neural validation using event-related potentials. *Behavior Research Methods* 42(3): 665–670.

Carlton, T. R. (1991). Introduction to the phonological history of the Slavic languages. Slavica Publishers, Inc, Columbus, Ohio.

[7] The licence of incom.py is freely available: https://github.com/uds-lsv/incompy.

Comrie, B. and Corbett, G. G. (1993). Introduction. In B. Comrie & G. G. Corbett (Eds.), *The Slavonic Languages*. Routledge, London/New York pp. 1–20.

Crocker, M., Demberg, V., and Teich, E. (2016). Information Density and Linguistic Encoding (IDeaL), *Künstliche Intelligenz* 30: 77–81.

Doyé, P. (2005). Intercomprehension. Guide for the development of language education policies in Europe: from linguistic diversity to plurilingual education. Reference study, Strasbourg, DG IV, Council of Europe.

Fischer, A., Jágrová, K., Stenger, I., Avgustinova, T., Klakow, D., and Marti, R. (2015). An orthography transformation experiment with Czech–Polish and Bulgarian–Russian parallel word sets. In B. Sharp, W. Lubaszewski & R. Delmonte, editors, Natural Language Processing and Cognitive Science 2015 Proceedings, pages 115–126, Libreria Editrice Cafoscarina, Venezia.

Fischer, A., Jágrová, K., Stenger, I., Avgustinova, T., Klakow, D., and Marti, R. (2016). Orthographic and Morphological Correspondences between Related Slavic Languages as a Base for Modeling of Mutual Intelligibility, Proceedings Language Resources and Evaluation Conference (LREC), pages 4202–4209, Portorož.

Golubović, J. (2016). Mutual intelligibility in the Slavic language area. PhD thesis. University of Groningen (Netherlands).

Gooskens, C. (2019). Receptive multilingualism. *Multidisciplinary perspectives on multilingualism: The fundamentals* LCB 19: 149–174.

Gooskens, C. (2007). The contribution of linguistic factors to the intelligibility of closely related languages. *Journal of Multilingual and Multicultural Development* 28(6): 445–467.

Gooskens, C. and van Heuven, V. J. (2019). How well can intelligibility of closely related languages in Europe be predicted by linguistic and non-linguistic variables? *Linguistic Approaches to Bilingualism*: 1–29.

Gooskens, C. and Swarte, F. (2017). Linguistic and extralinguistic predictors of mutual intelligibility between Germanic languages. *Nordic Journal of Linguistics* 40(2): 123–147.

Haugen, E. (1966). Semicommunication: The language gap in Scandinavia. *Sociological Inquiry* 36: 280–297.

van Heuven, V. J., Gooskens, C., and van Bezooijen, R. (2015). Introduction Micrela: Predicting mutual intelligibility between closely related languages in Europe. In: J. Navracsics & S. Batyi (Eds.), *First and Second Language: Interdisciplinary Approaches* (Studies in Psycholinguistics (6)), Tinta konyvkiado, Budapest, pp. 127–145.

Jágrová, K. and Avgustinova, T. (2019). Intelligibility of highly predictable Polish target words in sentences presented to Czech readers. To appear in Proceedings of CICLing: International Conference on Intelligent Text Processing and Computational Linguistics.

Jágrová, K., Avgustinova, T., Stenger, I., and Fischer, A. (2018). Language Models, Surprisal and Fantasy in Slavic Intercomprehension. In R. K. Moore, P. Fung & S. Narayanan (Eds.), *Computer Speech and Language* 53: 242–275.

Jágrová, K., Stenger, I., Marti, R., and Avgustinova, T. (2017). Lexical and orthographic distances between Bulgarian, Czech, Polish, and Russian: A comparative analysis of the most frequent nouns. In J. Emonds & M. Janebová (Eds.), Language Use and Linguistic Structure. Proceedings of the Olomouc Linguistics Colloquium 2016, pages 401–416, Palacký University, Olomouc.

Křen, M. (2010). Srovnávací frekvenční seznamy [Comparative frequency lists]. Prague: Institute of the Czech National Corpus Faculty of Arts, Charles University Prague. http://ucnk.ff.cuni.cz/index.php, accessed 2016-09-11.

Kürschner, S., van Bezooijen, R. and Gooskens, C. (2008). Linguistic determinants of the intelligibility of Swedish words among Danes. *International Journal of Humanities and Arts Computing* 2(1/2): 83–100.

Levenshtein, V. I. (1966). Binary Codes Capable of Correcting Deletions, Insertions and Reversals. *Soviet Physics Doklady* 10(8): 707–710.

Levy, R. (2008). Expectation-Based Syntactic Comprehension. *Cognition* 106(3): 1126–1177.

Likomanova, I. (2004). EuroComSlav Basiskurs – der internationale Wortschatz. http://www.eurocomslav.de/kurs/iwslav.htm, accessed 2016-02-17.

Ljaševskaja, O. N. and Šarov, S.A. (2009). Častotnyj slovar' sovremennogo russkogo jazyka [Frequency dictionary of the contemporary Russian language]. Moskva: Azbukovnik.

Mosbach, M., Stenger, I., Avgustinova T. and Klakow, D. (2019). incom.py – A Toolbox for Calculating Linguistic Distances and Asymmetries between Related Languages. In: G. Angelova, R. Mitkov, I. Nikolova & I. Temnikova, editors, Proceedings of Recent Advances in Natural Languages Processing (RANLP 2019), pages 811–819, Varna, Bulgaria.

Muikku-Werner, P. (2014). Co-text and receptive multilingualism Finnish students comprehending Estonian. *Journal of Estonian and Finno-Ugric Linguistics* 5(3): 99–103.

Ringbom, H. (2007). Cross-linguistic similarity in foreign language learning. Multilingual Matters LTD, Clevedon.

Shannon, C. E. (1948). A mathematical theory of communication. *Bell System Technical Journal* 27: (379–423), 623–656.

Stenger, I. (2019). Zur Rolle der Orthographie in der slavischen Interkomprehension mit besonderem Fokus auf die kyrillische Schrift. Dissertation. Universaar, Saarbrücken.

Stenger, I., Avgustinova, T., and Marti, R. (2017). Levenshtein distance and word adaptation surprisal as methods of measuring mutual intelligibility in reading comprehension of Slavic languages. Computational Linguistics and Intellectual Technologies: International Conference 'Dialogue 2017' Proceedings. Issue 16(23), vol. 1, pp. 304–317.

Stenger, I., Jágrová, K., Fischer, A., and Avgustinova, T. (2020). "Reading Polish with Czech Eyes" or "How Russian Can a Bulgarian Text Be?": Orthographic Differences as an Experimental Variable in Slavic Intercomprehension. In T. Radeva-Bork and P. Kosta (Eds.), *Current developments in Slavic Linguistics. Twenty years after. (based on selected papers from FDSL 11)*, Peter Lang, Bern, pp. 483–500.

Stenger, I., Jágrová, K., Fischer, A., Avgustinova, T., Klakow, D. and Marti, R. (2017). Modeling the impact of orthographic coding on Czech–Polish and Bulgarian–Russian reading intercomprehension. *Nordic Journal of Linguistics* 40(2): 175–199.

Vanhove, J. (2014). Receptive multilingualism across the lifespan. Cognitive and linguistic factors in cognate guessing. PhD thesis. University of Fribourg (Switzerland).

8. Language Resource References

incom.py – A toolbox for calculating linguistic distances and asymmetries between related languages. SFB 1102 – projects B4 and C4, available at: https://github.com/uds-lsv/incompy.

Intercomprehension Website (2014–2019). SFB 1102 – project C4 INCOMSLAV, availabe at: http://intercomprehension.coli.uni-saarland.de/de/.

Slavic Intecomprehension Matrix (2019). SFB 1102 – Project C4 INCOMSLAV, available at: http://intercomprehension.coli.uni-saarland.de/de/SlavMatrix/Results/.

Slavic Swadesh lists, https://en.wiktionary.org/wiki/Appendix:Slavic_Swadesh_lists, accessed on 2015-04-22.

Identifications of Speaker Ethnicity in South-East England: Multicultural London English as a Divisible Perceptual Variety

Amanda Cole
University of Essex
Department of Language and Linguistics
amanda.cole@essex.ac.uk

Abstract

This study uses crowdsourcing through LanguageARC to collect data on levels of accuracy in the identification of speakers' ethnicities. Ten participants (5 US; 5 South-East England) classified lexically identical speech stimuli from a corpus of 227 speakers aged 18-33yrs from South-East England into the main "ethnic" groups in Britain: White British, Black British and Asian British. Firstly, the data reveals that there is no significant geographic proximity effect on performance between US and British participants. Secondly, results contribute to recent work suggesting that despite the varying heritages of young, ethnic minority speakers in London, they speak an innovative and emerging variety: Multicultural London English (MLE) (e.g. Cheshire et al., 2011). Countering this, participants found perceptual linguistic differences between speakers of all 3 ethnicities (80.7% accuracy). The highest rate of accuracy (96%) was when identifying the ethnicity of Black British speakers from London whose speech seems to form a distinct, perceptual category. Participants also perform substantially better than chance at identifying Black British and Asian British speakers who are not from London (80% and 60% respectively). This suggests that MLE is not a single, homogeneous variety but instead, there are perceptual linguistic differences by ethnicity which transcend the borders of London.

Keywords: linguistic perception; linguistic variety identification; speaker ethnicity; MLE; Cockney; citizen linguistics, crowdsourcing

1. Introduction

1.1. Objective and subjective linguistic variation

There is a gap in linguistic research between what we know about language production and what we know about how language production is perceived and categorised. As explained by Clopper and Pisoni:

Despite large amounts of evidence to support the notion that linguistic variation between talkers due to regional and ethnic differences is real and robust and an important property of spoken language...we know less about what naïve listeners know about these sources of variation. (2007: 315 as cited in McKenzie, 2015).

Work in both perceptual phonetics (Clopper and Pisoni, 2007; Kendall and Fridland, 2010) and perceptual dialectology (Giles, 1970; Preston, 1989; Leach, Watson and Gnevsheva, 2016; Montgomery, 2012; Carrie and McKenzie, 2018) has sought to understand this knowledge gap which has implications, for example, when asking naïve listeners to provide judgements concerning the regional or social identity of speakers during annotation.

It has been established that listeners form categories which they assign speakers to depending on the speakers' linguistic forms and extra-linguistic information (Woolard, 2008; Eckert and Labov, 2017). As such, linguistic features can take on meaning as listeners begin to associate them with certain characteristics or social groups. In sociolinguistics, the term "indexicality" refers to the ideological relationship between linguistic features and a social group, persona, characteristic or place that they signal (see Silverstein 2003; Eckert 2008a). Linguistic features can move from having pre-ideological, social distributions to being indexing of macro-social groups such as class, gender, ethnicity or micro, local identities (e.g. "jocks" vs "burnouts" in Detroit: Eckert, 1989; see Silverstein's orders of indexicality 2003).

The social categories used by naïve listeners to define and categorise linguistic variation are not evenly distributed. For example, a study in North-East England asked British participants to listen to speech stimuli and identify where the speakers were from using their own labels (McKenzie, 2015). This work demonstrated that British participants have clear conceptions of what they perceive to be firstly, an Indian accent, secondly, the local, Tyneside accent and thirdly, a Scottish accent. Participants were mostly accurate at identifying speakers from these places. However, they did not hold categories say of "Thai" speech and were not able to accurately classify a Thai speaker.

In this sense, there are distinctions between subjective and objective boundaries. That is, the ways in which non-linguists categorise speakers may be distinct from true linguistic production (Preston, 2010). The disparity between subjective and objective linguistic variation can in part, be explained by both geographic proximity and cultural prominence. Geographic proximity effects have been found in listeners' ability to identify a speaker's home location (Montgomery, 2012). For instance, it is likely that a person from Liverpool will be more accurate than someone from Manchester at pin-pointing the home location of another Liverpool speaker based on their speech (Leach, Watson and Gnevsheva, 2016).

Nonetheless, geographic provenance alone is not sufficient to account for the perceptual labels formed and held by a community. In the above example in which Britons could accurately identify the speech of India but not Thailand, this is likely related to the shared social history, and thus, familiarity, between Britain and India (McKenzie, 2015). Indeed, despite a geographic distance of over 10,000 miles, Britons hold perceptual categories for vowel productions in New Zealand and Australian varieties of English (Shaw et al., 2019).

The language varieties spoken in some places are more easily identifiable than others due to the areas' higher cultural prominence (Montgomery, 2012; Montgomery and

Beal, 2011; Leach, Watson and Gnevsheva, 2016). Montgomery defines cultural prominence as follows:

Cultural prominence functions by bringing "far-away" areas "closer" to respondents through increased exposure in various forms of media and public discourse. (Montgomery, 2012: 640)

The level of cultural prominence associated with different places and their language varieties differs across communities. For instance, in Britain, the speech of India, Australia and New Zealand (amongst many other places) holds cultural prominence as a result of the countries' shared social history. Nonetheless, cultural prominence is not always bilateral. For instance, larger urban areas tend to have higher cultural prominence than rural areas (Leach, Watson and Gnevsheva, 2016). Furthermore, the level of cultural prominence that certain groups or locations hold is often mediated at least in part, by power relations.

Through draw-a-map tasks (Preston, 1989), Montgomery (2012) assessed British participants' mental knowledge of geographic variation within Britain. There is a power disparity between England and Scotland, for instance, England is the most notable seat of British political power. The study revealed that English participants often considered the entirety of Scotland to be one single speech zone, "Scottish". In contrast, Scottish participants identified as many distinct speech zones in England as the English participants (e.g. Cockney, West Country, etc.). Therefore, the categories formed by British participants was mediated by the relative cultural prominence of England and Scotland which in part, is reflected in the power relations between the two countries.

This section has summarised research into how speakers are categorised by listeners and how this can differ to the objective boundaries established in linguistic production research. This is partly conditioned by geographic proximity and cultural prominence effects. In this paper, I outline a LanguageARC project (see Cieri et al., 2018; 2019), *From Cockney to the Queen*, which examines how language in South-East England is produced, categorised and evaluated. In this paper, I present early results of one, single task from this project: an ethnicity identification task. This contributes to the very limited work on auditory identification of ethnicity (e.g. Todd, 2011a; Todd, 2011b).

This study analyses to what extent the perceptions of linguistic variation by ethnicity align with previous research on linguistic production in South-East England. As demonstrated in the following section, linguistic production has been shown to vary between ethnic minority and white speakers in London (e.g. Cheshire et al., 2011). Recent work suggests that despite the varying ethnic backgrounds and heritages of ethnic minority speakers in London, on the whole they speak a new and emerging variety of English: Multicultural London English (MLE) (Cheshire et al., 2011; Kerswill, Torgersen and Fox, 2008; Fox, 2015).

In this present study, participants were asked to categorise speakers from South-East England based solely on audio stimuli into the 3 main "ethnic" groups in Britain: White British, Black British and Asian British. I'll use the term "ethnicity" for these social groupings and treat them as emic or meaningful because they appear as such in public discourse and in government documents, while recognizing that the categories are troublesome from a scientific perspective.

In total, 10 participants took part, 5 of whom were based in the US and 5 in South-East England. Following the recent work on linguistic variation in London, we would predict that participants may be able to distinguish young, White British speakers from Asian British and Black British speakers, but will not find distinctive, linguistic differences between the latter two ethnicities. We would also expect a geographic proximity effect, such that speakers in the US are less accurate than speakers in South-East England.

Nonetheless, both these hypotheses are disconfirmed. The results reveal that firstly, there is no significant proximity effect. Secondly, participants perform at 80.7% accuracy, and have significantly higher rates of accuracy for Black British speakers whose speech seems to form a distinct, perceptual category.

1.2. The linguistic context: variation and change in London and South-East England

In the last few decades, South-East England and particularly, London have experienced much social and demographic change. In general, change in the South-East has been led by change initiated in London. Firstly, in what has been termed the "Cockney Diaspora", throughout more than 100 years, white working-class East Londoners have relocated to the home counties[1], and secondly, in the latter half of the 20th century, London experienced high rates of immigration (Watt, Millington and Huq, 2014; Fox, 2015; Butler and Hamnett, 2011; Young and Willmott, 1957; Cohen, 2013).

The Cockney Diaspora occurred as a result of many inter-related factors such as government-led slum clearance programmes between the 1920s and 1960s; a move to "better oneself" as East London had high rates of poverty; and the de-industrialisation of London (Watt, Millington and Huq, 2014; Fox, 2015; Butler and Hamnett, 2011; Young and Willmott, 1957; Cole and Strycharczuk, 2019; Cole and Evans, In Revision; Cohen, 2013). This led to a large-scale reduction in the White British population in London which has been termed by some as "White Flight" (Butler and Hamnett, 2011).

The county of Essex (which borders East London) has been the main out-post of the Cockney Diaspora and "White Flight" from London (Watt, Millington and Huq, 2014). Since the 1980s, the county has experienced increased economic and social mobility (Biressi and Nunn, 2013). Whilst previously, the border between outer London and Essex was most strongly demarcated by social class, in

[1] The home counties are the counties that immediately surround London.

modern times, it is increasingly a border of ethnicity (Butler and Hamnett, 2011: 8). Whilst the population of the white, working-class in London was still in decline in the latter half of the 20th century, the ethnic minority population began to rise rapidly in 1981. Between 1991 and 2011, London's ethnic minority population grew by 57% (Butler and Hamnett, 2011: 6). As a result, in modern times, East London is highly ethnically, culturally and linguistically diverse (Fox, 2015). For instance, in the 2011 census, the East London borough of Newham was the local authority in England and Wales where people from the White ethnic group made up the lowest percentage of the population (29%) (Office for National Statistics, 2011).

The large-scale social and demographic changes experienced in South-East England over previous decades have had linguistic consequences. Features of Cockney[2] are found to some extent, across South-East England (e.g. "Estuary English": Rosewarne, 1994), particularly, in outposts of the Cockney Diaspora to Essex (e.g. in Debden: Cole and Strycharczuk, 2019; Cole and Evans, In Revision). In the 1980s, Estuary English was first documented amongst those in their 20s and was perceived as a spectrum ranging from the standard variety, Received Pronunciation (RP), to Cockney that was found across South-East England (Rosewarne, 1994; Wells, 1997).

Wells (1992, 1997) considers Estuary English to share some features of Cockney such as t-glotalling in word-final position, vocalisation of pre-consonantal /l/ and yod-coalescence in stressed syllables, but to not have other features of Cockney such as h-dropping in content words, monophthongisation of the MOUTH vowel, th-fronting or inter-vocalic t-glotalling.

Estuary English was so named as it was perceived as being found most strongly along the Thames Estuary (Rosewarne, 1994), a stretch of water that runs eastward from the edge of London to the North Sea, delineating the county borders of Essex and Kent. It is no coincidence that many of the 20th century council estates erected to house Cockneys were built along the Thames Estuary. This includes the Becontree Estate in Dagenham, built between 1921 and 1935, which at completion comprised 24,000 homes and is still considered to be the largest municipal housing estate in Europe (London borough of Barking and Dagenham, 2014). Further, after the closure of the East London Docks in the 1970s, many dock workers relocated to the only remaining open docks, in Tilbury, Essex, on the Thames Estuary (Fox, 2015; Cohen, 2013).

Although Cockney linguistic features are found to some extent across South-East England and in particular, along the Thames Estuary, they are no longer found amongst young people in East London (Cheshire et al., 2008, 2011; Kerswill, Torgersen and Fox, 2008; Fox, 2015). Instead, in East and North London, a new variety of English, Multicultural London English (MLE), has emerged amongst young people as a result of contact between many different languages and dialects. Although the variety is found most strongly in inner-London, it appears to be diffusing outwards. For instance, it has been found to a lesser extent, in the outer East London borough of Havering (Cheshire et al., 2008, 2011).

This somewhat stigmatised variety of English (Fox and Kircher, 2019) is most strongly characterised by an innovative vowel system that does not share the diphthong shift which is a central feature of Cockney (Wells, 1982; Mott, 2012; Labov 1994). In relation to Cockney vowels, diphthongs are lowered and centralised in MLE (Kerswill, Torgersen and Fox, 2008).

Much work on MLE has categorised speakers in East London into "Anglo" and "non-Anglo"(Cheshire et al., 2011; Kerswill, Torgersen and Fox, 2008), defined respectively as "people of white British background and ... the children of immigrants, almost all from developing countries" (Kerswill and Torgersen, 2017: 17). This work has found that MLE is spoken most strongly by young, non-Anglo speakers in London, regardless of their ethnic background or heritage. Following this, participants may struggle to differentiate Asian British and Black British speakers in London, and perhaps, South-East England as a whole, as they are theoretically, speakers of a single dialect.

The above research has demonstrated that in South-East England, language varies by ethnicity, yet, this may also operate as a proxy for if a speaker is from London or the home counties. That is, ethnic minority speakers are indeed, most likely to use MLE features, but ethnic minority speakers are also most likely to live in London, where MLE is spoken. In the corpus of southern-eastern speech stimuli used in this project, 45.8% of Asian British and 74% of Black British speakers were from London, compared to 16.2% of White British speakers.

It is hard at this time to unpick whether MLE could be considered an ethnolect that is found to some extent in the speech of ethnic minority young people across South-East England (and perhaps beyond), or is a geographic dialect rooted most firmly in East London. To my knowledge, there has not been research into the extent to which MLE linguistic features are also used by ethnic minority speakers outside of London. However, it is known, that to a much lesser extent than ethnic minority speakers, MLE features are used by White British young people in inner-London, particularly those with ethnically mixed friendship networks (Cheshire et al., 2008; Fox, 2015). This poses the question: will participants only find perceptual linguistic differences between White British and non-White British speakers in London, but not in the remainder of the South-East?

This paper investigates subjective linguistic variation as well as how this relates to known, objective variation. This follows on from previous perceptual dialectology work in South-East England (Cole, Under Review). In this project, participants were found to associate ethnic minority speakers of MLE with East London and white, working-class speakers of near-Cockney with Essex, as found in a range of production studies (MLE: Cheshire et al., 2008,

[2] Cockney is the variety of English that has conventionally been associated with the white, working class in East London (Wells, 1982)

2011; Kerswill, Torgersen and Fox, 2008; Fox, 2015. Essex: Cole and Strycharczuk, 2019; Cole and Evans, In Revision). Nonetheless, participants' perceptual categories were not in complete alignment with the linguistic variation reported in production studies. Participants associated white, working-class speakers with not only Essex, but also East London in line with traditional associations, despite evidence that young speakers in East London no longer use Cockney features (Cheshire et al., 2008, 2011).

In this sense, it is not only of interest if participants can accurately identify a speaker's ethnicity, but also, the instances when they are incorrect. If listeners were to solely base their perceptual, linguistic categories on the linguistic variation which has been reported in production studies, we would firstly, expect them be able to distinguish most easily between white speakers who are not from London and non-white speakers who are from London. However, it seems unlikely that these categories will account for potential variation in the speech of White British speakers who live in London or ethnic minority speakers in the remainder of the South-East. Secondly, we would not expect participants to find distinctive differences between the speech of Asian British and Black British speakers. This paper reveals that participants do find perceptual differences between Asian British and Black British speakers, and the perceptual distinctions found between all 3 ethnicities transcend the borders of London.

2. Methods

This paper investigates to what extent participants can accurately identify young, south-eastern speakers as White British, Asian British or Black British in the context of ongoing linguistic change in South-East England. The research questions are the following:

1. Is there a geographic proximity effect in performance between US and British participants?
2. To what extent do participants' categorisations of speakers' ethnicities align with production research in South-East England?
    a. Will participants be able to distinguish White British speakers from Asian British and Black British speakers, but not find distinctive differences between the latter two ethnicities?
    b. Will participants only find perceptual linguistic differences between White British and non-White British speakers in London, but not in the remainder of the South-East?

This study is part of a wider project investigating how language in South-East England is used and perceived in relation to geographic location, class and ethnicity. This project, *From Cockney to the Queen*, has been set up on LanguageArc, an online resource which allows researchers to create language resources (Cieri et al., 2018, 2019). LanguageARC encourages members of the public, or Citizen Linguists, to spare as little or as much time as they would like to contribute to linguistic research.

The ethnicity identification task which will be discussed in this present paper is part of a series of 3 different task-types. In the first task-type, participants are asked to identify speakers' class, ethnicity or geographic location by selecting from fixed-term labels. In the second task-type, participants qualitatively describe their own class or ethnicity as well as what leads them to define it in this way. In the third task-type, participants qualitatively describe maps of either London or the South-East of England. They are asked to describe the distinct speech zones that they perceive in these areas as well as the demographics, characteristics and accents they would associate with each area. Participants perform the latter two tasks orally, by speaking aloud their answers which are recorded via their device's microphone and saved on storage managed by LanguageARC.

This study presents the results of the ethnicity identification task. In this task, 10 respondents from both the US and South-East England categorised speakers into the 3 most prevalent ethnicities in Britain according to the 2011 Census: White British, Asian British and Black British (Office for National Statistics, 2011). Whilst this project is at an early stage and further research will expand on this analysis, in general, little variation is found between the accuracies of each participant-group (US or South-East England), suggesting the findings may be robust despite low participants numbers.

2.1. Participants

A total of 10 respondents took part in the ethnicity identification task on LanguageARC. Of these respondents, 5 were based in Great Britain and 5 were based in the United States. The participants were not overtly recruited, but instead, participated in the task as part of their contribution more generally to LanguageARC. Given the geographic proximity effect, we would expect the participants in Great Britain to be more accurate at identifying the speakers' ethnicities than the participants in the US. Of the 5 respondents in Great Britain, LanguageARC recorded that they all completed the study in parts of South-East England (London, Oxford, Chelmsford and 2 respondents in Colchester). Of the respondents in the United States, 4 were in Philadelphia, Pennsylvania and 1 was in San Antonio, Texas. At this point, more information about the participants such as age, gender and ethnicity is not known.

2.2. Stimuli

Participants heard Speech stimuli taken from a corpus of 227 speakers from South-East England. The audio clips were lexically identical and were taken from a passage reading (Chicken Little: Shaw et al., 2018) which was recorded as part of a larger study on language production and perception in South-East England (Cole, Under Review). Although spontaneous speech would likely lead to greater use of vernacular features, a reading passage was chosen to control for contextual information or lexical choice. Each clip lasted approximately 10 seconds and was taken from a reading of the same sentence which was chosen to include a range of linguistic variables known to be variable between Cockney, MLE and RP:

"The sky is falling", cried Chicken Little. His head hurt and he could feel a big painful bump on it. "I'd better warn the others", and off he raced in a panicked cloud of fluff.

The speech stimuli were randomised for each individual participant. Each participant could complete as many or as few of the 277 judgements as they wished. The task did not have to be completed in one sitting, and participants could return to the task at any point and pick up where they left off. In fact, Citizen Linguists at LanguageARC are encouraged to dip into tasks even if they only wish to spare a few minutes.

All speakers were aged between 18 and 33 ($\overline{x}$ = 21.8; SD = 3.2). They had all lived in South-East England for at least half of the years between the ages of 3 and 18. The speakers came from a wide range of geographically disparate locations across South-East England, including within London. There was at least one speaker from each borough of London as well as the following counties: Bedfordshire, Cambridgeshire, Essex, Hertfordshire, Berkshire, Buckinghamshire, East Sussex, West Sussex, Hampshire, Norfolk, Suffolk, Surrey. Of the speakers, 41 identified as lower-working class, 54 as upper-working, 81 as lower-middle, 47 as upper-middle and 4 as upper class.

The stimuli were formed of 24 Asian British speakers, 54 Black British, 136 White British and 13 speakers who were categorised as "Other", as they did not fit into any of these 3 categories. For instance, if participants self-identified as "Kurdish" or "Mixed British" they were classified as "Other" for the purpose of this task. Judgements made about speakers in the "Other" category were not analysed in this present study which was interested in the identification of White British, Black British and Asian British speakers.

Speakers were asked to define their ethnicity in their own words. Following this, the speakers were grouped according to the most prevalent groups on the 2011 UK Census: White British, Black British and Asian British. For instance, a speaker who considered themselves "British Indian" was grouped as Asian British for the purpose of this study. Of the 54 speakers who were classified as Black British, 45 had self-identified using this term. Others had used terms such as "Black European", "Black Caribbean", "Black African" or "Black South African", but for the purpose of this study, were classified as "Black British".

Of the 136 White British participants, 134 had used this exact term in their self-identification of ethnicity, whilst 2 had identified as "White". Of the 24 Asian British speakers, only 9 had self-identified using this term whilst 15 were grouped as "Asian British" but had self-identified with terms such as "British Indian", "British Bangladeshi", "Pakistani British". This suggests that "Black British" and "White British" are important terms in speakers' own self-definition. However, although the term "Asian British" is used in popular discourse and official documentation, it may not capture the varied self-identifications amongst those grouped under this label.

In this study, I recognise that of course, ethnic identities are varied and complex (Hall-Lew, 2014). Indeed, language is a complex, symbolic resource used to communicate and infer social meaning and identity that extends far beyond ethnicity (Eckert, 2008b). For instance, it has long been established that in the US, not all speakers who are African American speak African American English (see Becker, 2014). Therefore, I would not expect, nor consider it possible, for participants to identify the ethnicity of all speakers with 100% accuracy. Nonetheless, this paper investigates to what extent these broad labels are salient and meaningful categories in terms of linguistic perception, and how this relates to previously reported linguistic production in South-East England.

2.3. Analysis

In total, 266 ethnicity judgements were made about speakers. Judgements were made about 119 of the 227 speakers. Of the 266 judgements, 189 were made by the British participants and 77 by the US participants. Of the 266 judgements, 26 judgements were made of Asian British speakers, 67 of Black British speakers and the remainder of White British speakers. When identifying a speaker's ethnicity, participants had the option to either select "Other" if they did not think the speaker belonged to any of the 3 choices provided, or they could skip that speaker. Participants did so on 2 and 17 instances respectively. These cases were not included in the analysis.

A logistic mixed effect regression was run in R using the glmer function of the lme4 package (Bates et al., 2015). This tested to what extent the gender, ethnicity and social class of speakers or the country of the participant (US or Great Britain) could predict the accuracy of the ethnicity judgements. Gender was included as it has been widely reported that men often use more vernacular features than women (see Labov's first principle, 1990). Social class was also included as it is an important determiner in linguistic variation in Britain (e.g. Milroy, 2001).

The dependent variable in the model was the participants' accuracy for each judgement: a two-level categorical variable coded as either "yes" or "no". White British was the reference level for the ethnicity variable, and lower-working class was the reference level for the social class variable. In order to control for the individual inputs of each participant, participant ID was included as a random intercept in the model. For all comparisons, α was set at 0.05.

3. Results

On the whole, respondents had reasonably high rates of accuracy when identifying the ethnicity of speakers, with an average of 80.7%. There were no significant effects for the participants' country, suggesting that there was not a proximity effect (US vs Great Britain: 78% and 81.6% accuracy respectively). There were also no significant effects of either speakers' social class (79.3%, 80%, 77.7%, 88.9% accuracy for lower-working, upper-working, lower-middle and upper-middle respectively) or gender (80.8% for male and 80.0% for female speakers).

Nonetheless, when a given speech stimuli was categorised by a participant, the resultant accuracy was dependent on the ethnicity of the speaker. The only significant effect found in the model was that Black British speakers were significantly more likely to be accurately assigned than White British speakers ($p = 0.005$). Participants accurately identified the ethnicity of Asian British speakers on 69.2%

of instances compared to 78% for White British speakers and 91.4% for Black British speakers (Fig. 1). The difference in accuracy between identifying White British and Asian British speakers was not found to be significant.

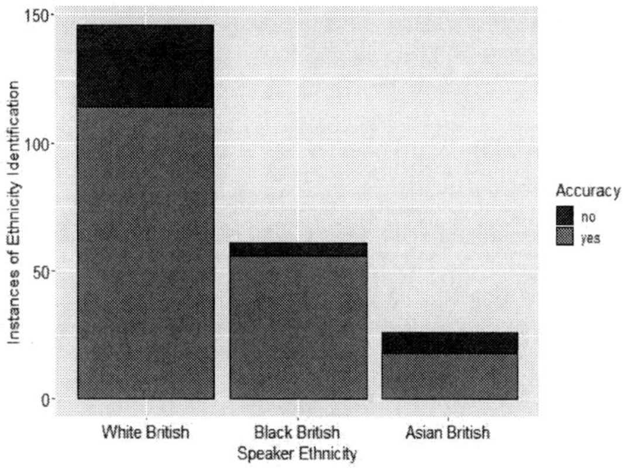

Figure 1: Accuracy of identifying a speaker's ethnicity based on speech stimuli. Black British speakers were significantly more likely to be accurately identified than Asian British or White British speakers.

On the instances in which participants inaccurately classed the stimuli (mis-identified a speaker's ethnicity), the relationship between the 3 ethnicities was not symmetrical (Fig. 2). Of the instances in which Asian British speakers were not accurately identified, they were considered to be White British on 87.5% of instances and Black British on 12.5% of occurrences. When White British participants were not correctly identified, they were judged to be Asian British on 59.4% of instances, and Black British on 40.6% of occurrences.

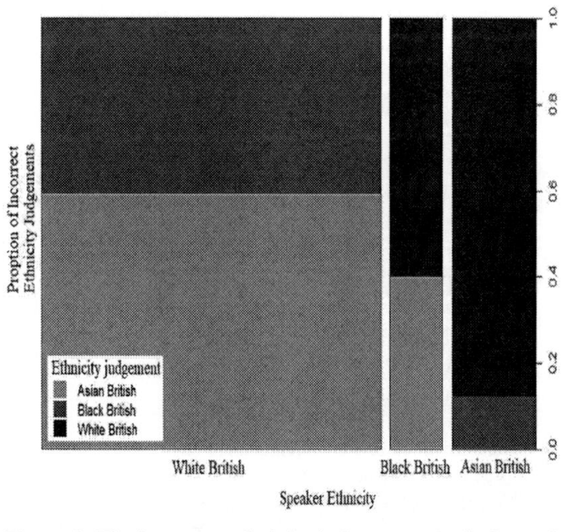

Figure 2: The incorrect ethnicity judgements made for each ethnicity group. When participants inaccurately label the ethnicity of Asian British or White British speakers, they frequently identify them as the other, but infrequently identify them as Black British. The column width reflects the uneven distribution of judgements made for speakers of each ethnicity in the data.

There is an overlap in how White British and Asian British speakers were identified such that they were most frequently mis-identified as the alternate group but were less frequently identified as Black British. The error made least frequently was identifying Asian British speakers as being Black British.

An analysis of the individual speakers whose ethnicity was most frequently identified either correctly or incorrectly sheds further light on the discrepancies between the 3 ethnicities. The findings suggest that for White British and Asian British speakers, their accent is associated with where they live as well as their ethnicity to a greater extent than for Black British speakers. The two speakers who were most frequently incorrectly identified were a White British speaker who lives in Ilford, East London and an Asian British participant who lives in Colchester, Essex. The former speaker was judged to be Asian British on 75% of instances, whilst the latter was judged to be White British on 75% of instances (n=4 for both).

Ilford is an area of London which is highly ethnically diverse and has a large Asian population. In the 2011 Census, in several wards in Ilford, British Indians formed around 25% of the population (Clementswood: 25.2%; Goodmayes: 24.5%; Valentines: 25.0%). In contrast, the Asian British speaker came from Colchester, a town in Northern Essex with low ethnic diversity (5.31% of the town's population were Asian British in the 2011 Census). The 15 Asian British participants who did not live in London were incorrectly categorised on 40% of instances, compared to 18% for the Asian British participants who lived in London. In contrast, the 28 White British participants who lived in London were inaccurately identified on 32.1% compared to 19.5% for those who did not live in London.

This is not to say that Black British speakers from across South-East England were identified with equal accuracy. The Black British participants who lived in London were inaccurately identified on only 4% of instances, compared to 20% amongst those who did not live in London. It seems that Black British speakers in London speak a variety of English that is perceptually, very distinct. Indeed, the 2 speakers whose ethnicities were most frequently accurately identified were a Black British speaker in East London and a White British speaker who lives in Rochester, on the Thames Estuary (100% accuracy, n=12 and n=5 respectively). The former location has a high prevalence of MLE (Cheshire et al., 2008, 2011), whilst the latter location is on the Thames Estuary, the area most strongly associated with Estuary English (Rosewarne, 1994). Therefore, it may be little surprise that these speakers had accents that led them to be accurately identified as their respective ethnicities on 100% of instances.

4. Discussion

This study aimed to contribute to the gap in linguistic research between what we know about language production and what we know about how language production is perceived and categorised (McKenzie, 2015; Clopper and Pisoni, 2007; Preston, 2010). This study used LanguageARC to collect data from Citizen Linguists to analyse levels of accuracy in the identification of speakers' ethnicities.

The data revealed that firstly, a geographic proximity effect was not found. There were no significant differences in performance between participants in South-East England and the US. The lack of a proximity effect in this study may be attributable to several reasons. Previous studies on geographic proximity have investigated participants' ability to identify a speaker's geographic provenance. It has been found that participants perform better if they are from nearby the speaker (Leach, Watson and Gnevsheva, 2016; Montgomery, 2012). Nonetheless, this present study investigated participants' performance in identifying speakers' ethnicity, not geographic provenance, which may not be constrained by geographic proximity to the same extent. This is in line with previous research which found that a listener's performance at identifying speakers' ethnicity did not continually improve with repeated (task) exposure (Todd, 2011b).

It may be that there was not a significant proximity effect as a result of the nature of ethnolects. Previous work has suggested that ethnolects are marked by substrate influences from speakers' L1s (or heritage L1s) during the period of transition from bilingualism to monolingualism in the L2 (Clyne, 2000; Wolck, 2002). Therefore, regardless of whether the L2 is a variety of American English or British English, the ethnolects spoken in these respective countries may be marked by linguistic features found in the (heritage) L1s of ethnic minority speakers. Thus, a familiarity with British Englishes may not be the key determiner in performance at this task. It may also be the case that US speakers are more finely attuned to ethnic linguistic differences as ethnicity takes precedence in linguistic ideology in the US whilst social class is central to British linguistic ideology (Milroy, 2001).

As well as investigating geographic proximity effects, this paper examined to what extent the 3 ethnicities were perceptual categories held by the listeners. It has been established that individuals categorise people that they encounter based in part, on the speakers' linguistic output. The labels that listeners use in their categorisation of language varieties is dependent on both the distinct social sphere of a community (Woolard, 2008; Eckert and Labov, 2017) and the listener's familiarity with the language variety (e.g. cultural prominence: Montgomery, 2012; Montgomery and Beal, 2011; Leach, Watson and Gnevsheva, 2016). This study found that Black British is a meaningful linguistic category in linguistic perception. This is not to say that Asian British and White British are not also meaningful, linguistic categories. Indeed, on the whole, participants performed the task with relatively high accuracy (80.7%), but participants were significantly more accurate in classifying speakers who were Black British than Asian British or White British.

It may be the case that the labels "Asian British" and "White British" cannot fully capture the linguistic variation found within these groups. However, it is also possible that these varieties are as linguistically distinct and relatively homogeneous as Black British, but that participants do not hold such well-defined perceptual categories for these varieties. When self-defining their ethnicity with free classification, "Black British" and in particular, "White British" were terms that were widely used by speakers. In contrast, "Asian British" was highly divisible in the speakers' self-identification (e.g. "British Indian", "British Bangladeshi", "Pakistani British"). This adds weight to the interpretation that although participants hold a perceptual category for "White British" speech, there is more variation in the speech of south-eastern White British speakers than is captured within this perceptual category. In contrast, whilst there is most likely, also relative variation in the speech of Asian British speakers, it seems that listeners do not hold such a clear perceptual category for "Asian British" speech.

When participants inaccurately classed the ethnicity of Asian British or White British speakers, they frequently identified them as the alternate group, but infrequently identified them as Black British. This was particularly the case for Asian British speakers who were relatively infrequently identified as Black British (3.8% of all judgements). There is not an equal distribution of misses across all classifications. White British participants could be mis-identified as Black British or Asian British (but more frequently the latter); Black British participants could be identified as either Asian British or more frequently, White British; Asian British participants were almost only ever mis-categorised as White British and not Black British.

In part, the rates of misidentification are related to the speakers' geographic provenance. Asian British and Black British speakers who lived outside of London were more frequently mis-identified than those who lived in London. In contrast, White British speakers who lived in London were more frequently mis-identified than those who did not live in London. The effect was not as large for Black British speakers as the other two ethnicities. It seems that many Black British speakers speak in a perceptually similar way across South-East England. This way of speaking is most strongly associated with London.

Black British speakers in London were almost never mis-identified as a different ethnicity (4% of instances), suggesting that the variety of English spoken by this group in London is perceptually, very distinct. Nonetheless, the rates of accurate identification were greater than chance for both Asian British and Black British speakers who were not from London (60% and 80% respectively). This suggests that to some extent, perceptual linguistic differences by ethnicity are found across South-East England. Although the varieties of English associated with Black British and Asian British speakers are most strongly rooted in London, they are not limited to the city.

This study has contributed to work on language variation and change in South-East England. Following work on MLE (Cheshire et al., 2008, 2011; Kerswill, Torgersen and Fox, 2008), I predicted that participants may be able to distinguish White British speakers from Asian British and Black British speakers, but would not find distinctive, linguistic differences between the latter two ethnicities. The results reveal that speakers had relatively high levels of accuracy at distinguishing between all 3 ethnicities, but in particular, the speech of Black British speakers seems to form a distinct, perceptual category.

Furthermore, White British speakers were most easily identified if they did not live in London, and the reverse was found for Asian British and Black British speakers. Nonetheless, listeners performed much better than chance at identifying the ethnicity of speakers from all locations in the South-East. This perceptual evidence suggests that MLE is most strongly but not exclusively found in London. Many Black British and Asian British speakers from across South-East England use linguistic features that perceptually mark out their ethnicity. This paper concludes that MLE is not a single, homogeneous variety but instead, there are perceptual linguistic differences by ethnicity which transcend the borders of London.

5. References

Bates, D. Maechler, M. Bolker, B. and Walker, S. (2015). Fitting Linear Mixed-Effects Models Using lme4. *Journal of Statistical Software*, 67(1):1-48.

Becker, K. (2014). Linguistic repertoire and ethnic identity in New York City. In L. Hall-Lew and M. Yaeger-Dror (Eds.) *New Perspectives on Linguistic Variation and Ethnic Identity in North America. Special issue of Language and Communication* 35:43-54.

Biressi, A. and Nunn, H. (2013). Essex: Class, Aspiration and Social Mobility. In A. Biressi & H. Nunn (Eds.), *Class and Contemporary British Culture.* Palgrave Macmillan, London, pp. 23-43.

Butler, T. and Hamnett, C. (2011). *Ethnicity, class and aspiration: understanding London's new East End.* Policy Press.

Carrie, E. and McKenzie, R. M. (2018). American or British? L2 speakers' recognition and evaluations of accent features in English. *Journal of Multilingual and Multicultural Development*, 39(4):313-328.

Cheshire, J., Fox, S., Kerswill, P. and Torgersen, E. (2008). Ethnicity, friendship network and social practices as the motor of dialect change: linguistic innovation in London. *Sociolinguistica,* 22(1):1–23.

Cheshire, J., Kerswill, P., Fox, S. and Torgersen, E., (2011). Contact, the feature pool and the speech community: the emergence of Multicultural London English. *Journal of Sociolinguistics*, 15(2):151–196.

Cieri, C., Fiumara, J., Liberman, M., Callison-Burch, C., and Wright, J. (2018). Introducing NIEUW: Novel Incentives and Workflows for Eliciting Linguistic Data *Proceedings of the 11th Edition of the Language Resources and Evaluation Conference (LREC 2018).* Pages 151-155, Miyazaki, May 7-12.

Cieri, C., Write, J., Fiumara, J., Shelmire, A. and Liberman, M. (2019). LanguageARC: Using Citizen Science to Augment Sociolinguistic Data Collection and Coding *NWAV48: New Ways of Analyzing Variation Eugene*, October 10-12.

Clopper, C. G. and Pisoni, D. B. (2007). Free classification of regional dialects of American English. *Journal of phonetics*, 35(3):421-438.

Clyne, M. (2000). Lingua franca and ethnolects in Europe and beyond. *Sociolinguistica*, 14(1):83–89.

Cohen, P. (2013). *On the Wrong Side of the Track? East London and the Post Olympics*. London: Lawrence & Wishart.

Cole, A. Under Review. Perceived linguistic variation by class, ethnicity and geography in Southeast England: the digitalisation of the perceptual dialectology paradigm.

Cole, A. and Evans, B. (In Revision). Phonetic variation and change in the Cockney Diaspora: the role of place, gender and identity

Cole, A. and Strycharczuk, P. (2019). The PRICE-MOUTH crossover in the 'Cockney diaspora'. In S.Calhoun, P. Escudero, M.Tabain & P.Warren (Eds.), *Proceedings of the 19th International Congress of Phonetic Sciences (ICPhS),* pages 602-606, Melbourne, Australia 2019.

Eckert, P. (1989). *Jocks and burnouts: Social categories and identity in the high school.* Teachers college press.

Eckert, P. (2008a). Variation and the indexical field. *Journal of sociolinguistics,* 12(4):453-476.

Eckert, P. (2008b). Where do ethnolects stop?. *International Journal of Bilingualism*, 12(1-2):25-42.

Eckert, P. and Labov, W. (2017). Phonetics, phonology and social meaning. *Journal of Sociolinguistics,* 21(4):467-496.

Fox, S. (2015). *The new Cockney: New ethnicities and adolescent speech in the traditional East End of London.* Basingstoke: Palgrave Macmillan.

Giles, H. (1970). Evaluative reactions to accents. *Educational review,* 22(3):211-227.

Hall-Lew, L. and Yaeger-Dror, M. (2014). New perspectives on linguistic variation and ethnic identity in North America. *Language & Communication,* 35:1-8.

Kendall, T. and Fridland, V. (2010). Mapping production and perception in regional vowel shifts. *University of Pennsylvania Working Papers in Linguistics,* 16(2):101:112

Kerswill, P. Torgersen, E. and Fox, S. (2008). Reversing "drift": Innovation and Diffusion in the London Diphthong System. *Language Variation and Change.* 20(3):451–491.

Kerswill, P. and Torgersen, E. (2017). London's Cockney in the twentieth century: Stability or cycles of contact-driven change? In R.Hickey (Ed.), *Listening to the Past.* Cambridge University Press, Cambridge, pp.85-113

Kircher, R. and Fox, S. (2019). Multicultural London English and its speakers: a corpus-informed discourse study of standard language ideology and social stereotypes. *Journal of Multilingual and Multicultural Development*, 1-19.

Labov, W. (1990). The intersection of sex and social class in the course of linguistic change. *Language Variation and Change*, 2(2):205-254

Labov, W. (1994). *Principles of Linguistic Change.* Blackwell.

Leach, H., Watson, K. and Gnevsheva, K. (2016). Perceptual dialectology in northern England: Accent recognition, geographical proximity and cultural prominence. *Journal of Sociolinguistics,* 20(2):192-211.

London Borough of Barking and Dagenham. (2014). *The Becontree Estate Information Sheet.*

McKenzie, R. M. (2015). The sociolinguistics of variety identification and categorisation: Free classification of varieties of spoken English amongst non-linguist listeners. *Language Awareness*, 24(2):150-168.

Milroy, L. (2001). Britain and the United States: Two nations divided by the same language (and different language ideologies). *Journal of Linguistic Anthropology*, 10(1):56-89.

Montgomery, C. (2012). The effect of proximity in perceptual dialectology. *Journal of Sociolinguistics*, 16(5):638-668.

Montgomery, C. and Beal, J. (2011). *Perceptual Dialectology*. Cambridge University Press.
Mott, B. L. (2012). Traditional Cockney and popular London speech. Dialectologia, 9:69-94.
Office for National Statistics. (2011). UK Census 2011
Preston, D. (1989). *Perceptual Dialectology. Nonlinguists' Views of Areal Linguistics*. Foris, Dordrecht, Providence.
Preston, D. (2010). Language, people, salience, space: perceptual dialectology and language regard. *Dialectologia*, (5):87-131.
Rosewarne, D. (1994). Estuary English: tomorrow's RP?. *English today,* 10(1):3-8.
Shaw, J. A., Best, C. T., Docherty, G. J., Evans, B. G., Foulkes, P., Hay, J. and Mulak, K. (2018). Resilience of English vowel perception across regional accent variation. *Laboratory Phonology,* 9(1):1-36
Silverstein, M. (2003). Indexical order and the dialectics of sociolinguistic life. *Language & Communication*, 23(3-4):193-229.
Todd, R. (2011a). Identifications of speaker-ethnicity: Attribution accuracy in changeable settings. In *Fourth ISCA Workshop on Experimental Linguistics*. pp.135-138.
Todd, R., (2011b). Ethnic Group Attribution: Is Our Reliability Constrained by Time Spent with Others? In *Proceedings of the 17th International Congress of Phonetic Sciences (ICPhS),* pages 1998-2001, Hong Kong 2011.
Watt, P. Millington, G. and Huq, R. (2014). East London Mobilities: The 'Cockney Diaspora' and the Remaking of the Essex Ethnoscape. In P.Watt & P.Smets, (Eds.) *Mobilities and Neighbourhood Belonging in Cities and Suburbs*, Palgrave Macmillan UK, pp. 121-144.
Wells, J. C. (1982). *Accents of English*. Cambridge: Cambridge University Press.
Wells, J. C. (1992). Estuary English?!?. *BAAP Colloquium,* Cambridge.
Wells, J. C. (1997). What is Estuary English. *English Teaching Professional*, 3:46-47.
Wolck, W. (2002). Ethnolects – between bilingualism and urban dialect. In J.A. Fishman (Ed.) *Opportunities and Challenges of Bilingualism*. Pages 157-170, Mouton de Gruyter, Berlin.
Woolard, K. A. (2008). Why dat now?: Linguistic-anthropological contributions to the explanation of sociolinguistic icons and change. *Journal of Sociolinguistics*, 12(4):432-452.
Young, M. and Willmott, P. (1957) *Family and Kinship in East London*. Routledge and Kegan Paul, London.

Proceedings of the LREC 2020 Workshop "Citizen Linguistics in Language Resource Development", pages 58–61
Language Resources and Evaluation Conference (LREC 2020), Marseille, 11–16 May 2020

LanguageARC – a tutorial

Christopher Cieri, James Fiumara
University of Pennsylvania, Linguistic Data Consortium
3600 Market Street, Philadelphia, PA 19104 USA
{ccieri, jfiumara}@ldc.upenn.edu

Abstract

LanguageARC is a portal that offers citizen linguists opportunities to contribute to language related research. It also provides researchers with infrastructure for easily creating data collection and annotation tasks on the portal and potentially connecting with contributors. This document describes LanguageARC's main features and operation for researchers interested in creating new projects and or using the resulting data.

Keywords: language resources, crowd-sourcing, citizen linguistics

1. Introduction

LanguageARC is a portal that connects researchers to citizen linguists who may be interested in contributing to research projects (Figure 1). It was created as part of the NIEUW project which investigates novel incentives in the elicitation of language related data as a way to fill the gaps in available language resources left by other approaches.

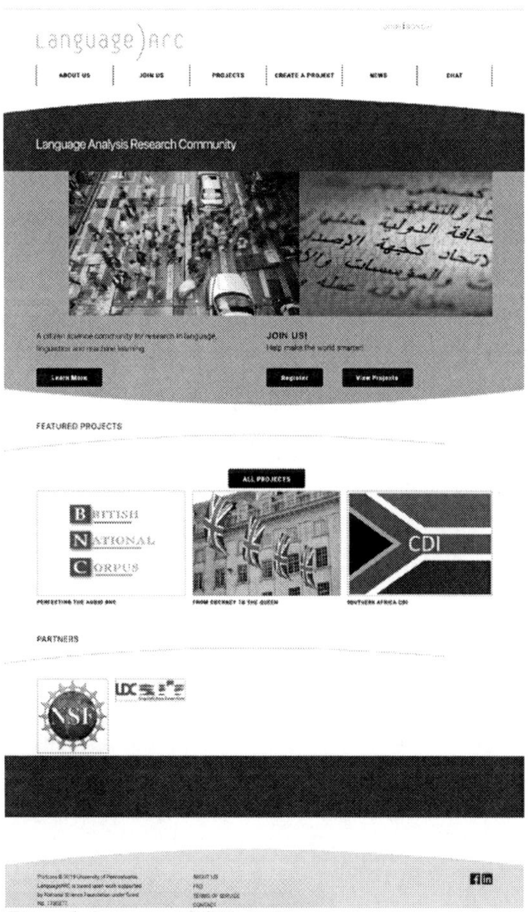

Figure 1: LanguageARC Home Page

Other NIEUW outcomes include the language games portal LingoBoingo.org and the language identification game NameThatLanguage.org which offer the incentives of entertainment, competition and opportunities to learn in exchange for language data. In contrast, LanguageARC offers members of the public interested in language (citizen linguists) opportunities to learn about and make direct contributions to research on language and to join groups of like-minded contributors.

LanguageARC includes a project builder that vastly simplifies the steps required to create and deploy a cluster of related web pages that collect data and annotation. Two design goals are that: 1) tasks should be simple and short enough to be completed by citizen linguists, for example, while commuting, on a work break, waiting for an order in a restaurant, etc. and 2) that researchers should be able to implement new tasks in less than one hour given a design and data in the appropriate format. These design goals are intended to lower the barriers to participation for both researchers and citizen linguists.

2. Terminology

LanguageARC's principal organizing scheme is that the portal hosts multiple *projects*, each of which contains one or more *tasks*, each of which iterates over one or more *items*. A *project* is a set of tasks organized by a research team to support a specific research goal. LanguageARC tasks are organized by project – rather than, for example, by language, activity type or application – to give research teams the opportunity to describe their work in a way that attracts citizen linguist *contributors*. To appeal to contributors, a project has a compelling *project image*, *title*, *call to action* and *description*. Each project is represented by a *card* on LanguageARC's multi-page grid of all projects (see Figure 2). The card displays the project's image, title and call to action. Clicking any card takes the user to that project's *main page*.

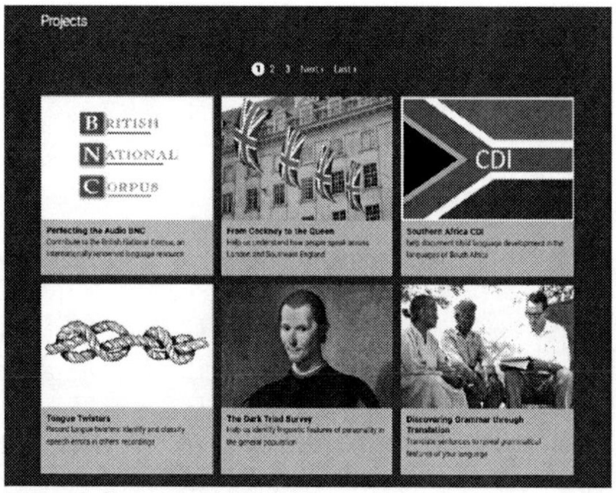

Figure 2: Project grid (partial)

The project main page (Figure 4) repeats the project title, call to action and image but also adds a *description*, optional *partner badges* and optional links to *News*, *Chat* and *Research Team* pages. Currently, there is no blog implemented within the portal but projects that have their own external blog or web pages can use the News link to connect contributors to those. LanguageARC does have its own discussion groups accessible via the Chat link. The project main page also contains a large button that reads *Start Now* for new contributors and *Continue* for returning contributors.

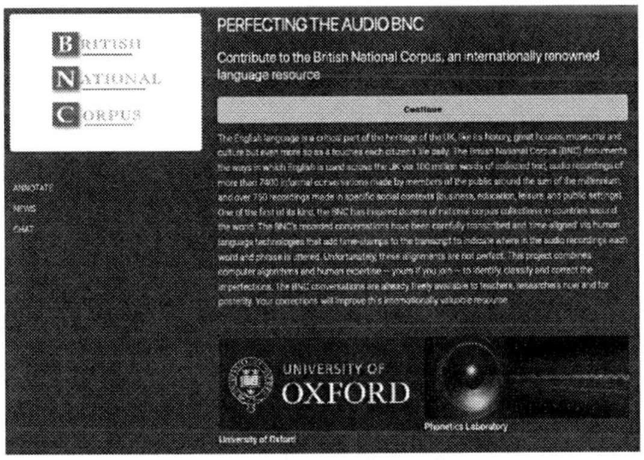

Figure 4: One project's main page (partial)

Every project must have at least one task but projects can have many more than one. If a project has multiple tasks, the Start Now/Continue button takes the contributor to the *task list* (Figure 5); otherwise it starts the single task immediately. The task list page inherits any Research Team, News and Chat links from the project main page but add an image, title, call to action and Start/Continue button for each task within the project. Clicking the Start/Continue button for any task takes the contributors to the tasks tool page.

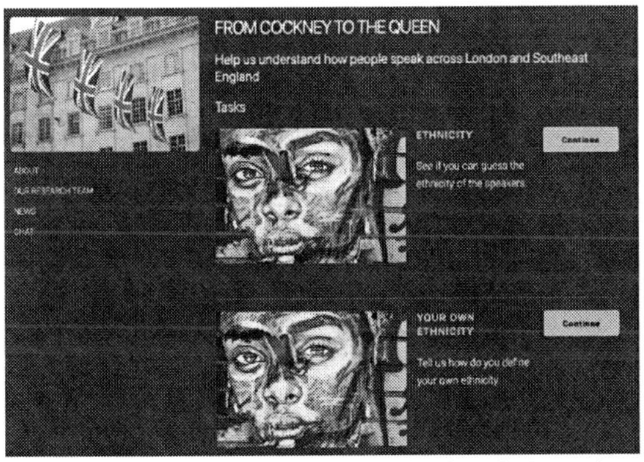

Figure 5: Task list for a project with multiple tasks (partial)

Each task has one and only one *tool* page (see Figure 3). This is where most of the work is done. The tool is built from widgets or controls, customized for the task, that allow the contributor to play audio or video, read text or view images and then contribute language data by typing or recording themselves speaking responses or by clicking buttons. Each tool page can include optional links to a *tutorial* and *reference guide*. Each task performs the same action over one or more items in a data set. A *data set* is defined as a *manifest* that enumerates a set of items by providing identifiers for each item as well as item specific texts, media files or both. Media files can be text, audio, image or video.

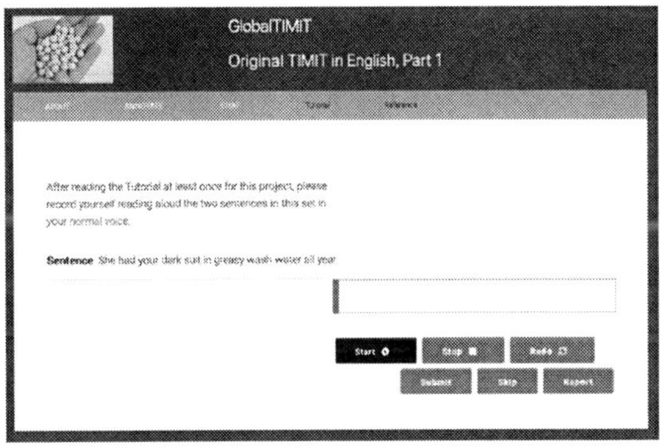

Figure 3: Tool page (partial)

3. Preparing a Project

Before beginning implementation, *project designers* consider their research goals and the subset of tasks citizen linguists could do. Citizen scientists contributing to other portals such as *Zooniverse* have demonstrated their willingness to learn complex tasks and ability to complete them with high quality. Nevertheless, it remains the case that human performance is better for straightforward tasks with clear instructions that require contributors to make one kind of decision at a time. For example, if the research required both collecting transcripts and judgments about the pronunciation of audio segments, the project designer would divide that effort into two tasks. LanguageARC reflects this approach by holding the tool and instructions constant across all items within in a task.

Once the project designer has defined collection and annotation, the next step is to segment any media into the units over which decisions are to be made. For example if the research goal were to transcribe conversations, the project designer would first divide the conversation into e.g. pause groups (of 4 to 8 seconds duration) which would likely require 1-2 minutes to transcribe, about the right length for a single item.

With tasks defined and media segmented, the next step is to create a manifest. A manifest is a text file of all of the items to be collected or annotated, with each item on its own line and columns separated by tab characters. Those items will be presented to citizen linguists one at a time in the tool. The manifest must always have an identifier for each item and either one or two *item specific texts* or a media file name or both. Thus a minimal manifest has two columns and a maximal one has four.

Item identifiers are required as they link the items in the manifest to the citizen linguist contributions in the automatically generated reports. The identifier can be any string of characters including a second copy of the media file name. Most projects to date have used a simple numeric counter.

Manifest files can be built from a spreadsheet that has each item in a row with the ID, item specific text and media file names in spreadsheets columns by saving the spreadsheet in the TSV (tab separated values) format. A project designer could also create a manifest directly using a plain text editor (not a Word Processor) by placing each item on its own line with tab characters separating the ID, item specific text and media file names. columns. In the latter case, project designers should assure that the text editor is inserting actual tabs and not sequences of space characters.

With the manifest complete, the next consideration is training. LanguageARC project designers can associate a separate tutorial and reference guide with each task. In projects created so far, the tutorial introduces the task, provides any background information needed and describes the decision or other contribution to be made and perhaps repeated. The reference guides normally include screenshots of the interface with explanations, examplars of annotation categories, definitions of terminology and acknowledgments, e.g. to people who have provided media used in building the task.

To expedite implementation, project designers gather media files to annotates and any supplemental media used in the training materials, create the manifest file and write instructions in advance of using the project builder.

Before a researcher can create LanguageARC projects, they must be given credentials as a project designer which they can request from the authors. A researcher logs into an authorized LanguageARC account will see a *Create Project* button in the main menu. Project designers can create new projects, multiple tasks within those projects and datasets for use by those tasks. They can also invite collaborators to join their projects as *task designers*, with power to edit specific tasks, or as *other contributors*. Within a **task**, task designers have all the power of project designers but cannot change **project** details or create new tasks. To avoid being tedious, we will use "project designer" below but the reader should interpret this to include "task designers" when we are discussing creating or editing task elements. *Other contributors* refers to the subset of LanguageARC contributors who have been invited, and thus have access, to a specific project or task before it is published. Finally, project designers can run reports of all contributions made to their tasks. After the project designer has tested a project and its tasks and believes it ready for public access, they use the project builder to send a request to LanguageARC *portal managers* that the project be published. Portal managers review the project to assure that it is appropriate in goals and content and that no sensitive personally identifiable information is requested. Once published, the project is available to any member of the public who creates a LanguageARC account.

4. Creating a Project

As above, preparing material in advance expedites the implementation of a LanguageARC project. Projects require an internal name, title, call to action, image and description. Not required but strongly suggested are the page about the research team and partner badges which may help attract contributors. Projects can optionally include links to an external blog or website and any of four forums associated with the project.

The *internal name* of the project is what will appear in the project builder. It need only be globally unique (not used elsewhere in LanguageARC) and memorable to the designer. The project *title* is displayed prominently on the project main page and on the project card that appears in the grid. This title must be globally unique and should be both descriptive and attractive to potential collaborators. The *call to action*, also called the subtitle in the project builder, is normally a short phrase requesting the contributions of citizen linguists, again in a way that is compelling.

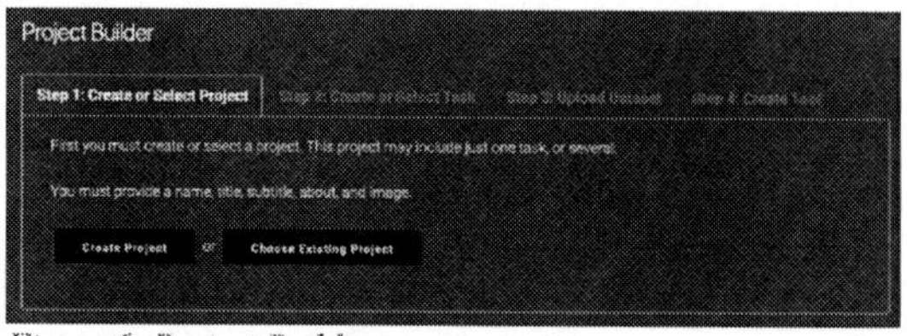

Figure 6: Project Builder

The project *description*, labeled "about your project and tasks" in the project builder, is typically a paragraph briefly describing the project research goals, how citizen linguists can help and what they will be asked to do. Where the previous fields could hold only plain text, this field accepts markdown, described in §5, to allow e.g. the use of links. Although a markdown capable field allows it, good design principles argue against complex formatting in the description given the space available. If the project has an external blog or web page, this can be entered in the News/Blog field and then reached via a News link.

Like the title, the project image should be representative of the project but also compelling to potential contributors. In addition, the project image should have an aspect ratio of 2 units high by 3 wide; that is, if the image were 200 pixels high it should be 300 pixels wide. Any multiple of 2x3 will display nicely however, images larger than 600 by 900 pixels will be scaled down (thus a waste of storage) while any smaller than ~ 200 x 300 will be scaled up and appear pixelated.

Project assets are media files uploaded not for annotation but to be included in e.g. the tutorial or reference guide.

Project designers can activate any of four discussion forums for their projects. The intended uses of the project forums are probably clear from their names. We anticipate that researchers will announce changes to the project, papers accepted, press coverage and other successes resulting from the use of project data in the Announcements forum. The *General Discussion* forum will most likely be populated by citizen linguists who discuss the project with each other. If the *Questions for Research Team* forum is activated then ideally the research team would monitor this on a regular basis and answer any questions arising from citizen linguists. Finally we have included a *Help and Technical Support* forum observing that in other citizen science portals, contributors often support each other which reduces the burden on the research team. Naturally, it would be wise to monitor this forum in case incorrect advice were given.

The *Research Team Members* section is a separate page, accessible from the project main page, that provides the names, titles, brief biosketches and images for the researchers who have developed the project. Similarly the Partner Badges section allows project designers to add the name, image and linked URL for each organizational partner. These appear at the bottom of the project main page. Typically the image is a logo and links to the partner's homepage.

With this information prepared, a researcher logs into LanguageARC using their account, which has previously been authorized as a project designer and clicks the Create a Project to access the Project Builder. The dialog box in Figure 6 will appear showing four tabs, the first labeled *Step 1: Create or Select Project* should be highlighted

Clicking "Create Project opens the New Project form in Figure 8. Only after completing this form, the project designer clicks Save.

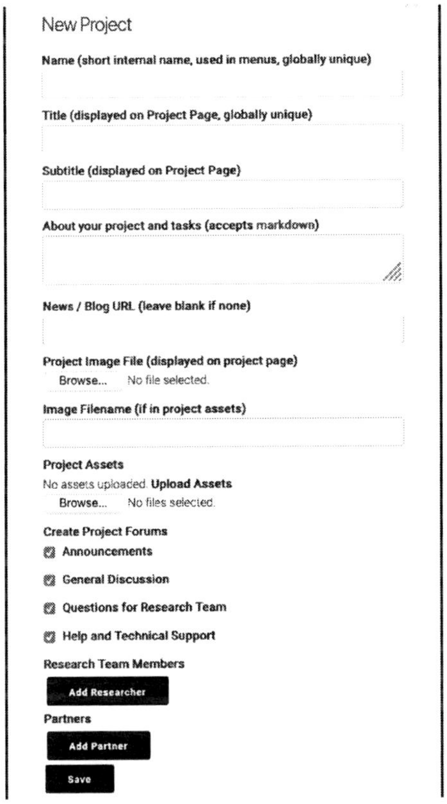

Figure 8: New Project form

A few seconds later a dialog box should appear saying: *Project created or selected successfully.* Clicking the X dismisses the dialog box. Any information entered in Step 1 can be edited later, as described below.

5. Creating Tasks within a Project

If all has gone well so far, the project builder should have highlighted the tab *Step 2: Create or Select Task.* Clicking *Create Task* opens the *New Task* form shown in Figure 7.

Several fields on the New Task form will be familiar. A task requires an internal name, a title and call to action (labelled task description) that will appear on the project's task list. Next, project designers can enter the contents of their *tutorial* and *reference guide*. Both of these open in new browser windows, giving the project designer more freedom in formatting. Both accept markdown that can be used to insert formatting, links and media into the text following the specification linked from that form.[1] LanguageARC adds one new feature to the markdown specification: any file uploaded to the project assets can be inserted into any markdown capable field by surrounding it with *{local}* tags, e.g. {local}MyAudio.wav{local}.

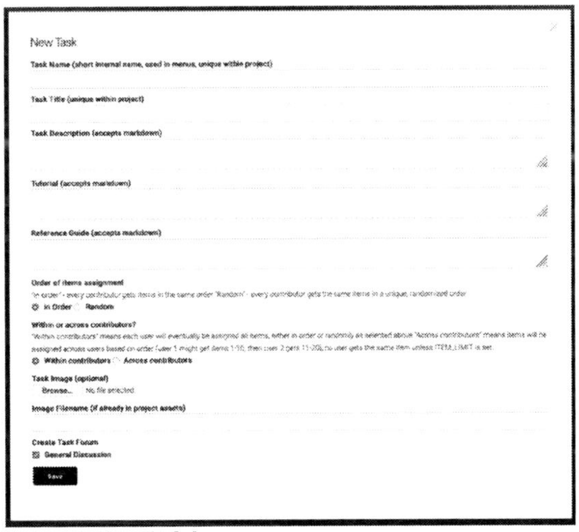

Figure 7: New Task form

The next three fields require some explanation. With *Order of item assignment*, project designers can choose between assigning items in the order that they appeared in the manifest file or randomized uniquely for each contributor. If random is chosen, a second question will appear asking whether to allow repeats. Essentially, those are asking whether to performs the randomization with or without replacement. If *Repeating* is checked any single user may see some items multiple times before seeing all items in the data set.

The next question concerns whether to assign items within or across contributors. The former means that if a user were to see as many items as there are in the manifest they would actually have seen every item in the manifest. The latter means that the first batch of items will be given to the first contributor, and the next batch to the next contributor who requests them. In a task that had only one contributor, these would have the same effect. However if a second contributor joins the task before the first contributor has finished the first batch of annotations then the second contributor will receive the second batch. Various combinations of these choices allow a project designer to e.g. maximize the number of items that receive at least one imitation or to maximize the number of annotations an item receives.

The next two fields are familiar. A project designer may associate an image with the task that is different from the project image and from all other task images and may create a *General Discussion* forum specific to the task even if a General Discussion forum was created for the project as a whole. Only when the entire form is complete, the project designer clicks Save. If all goes well, a dialog box will appear saying; *Task created or selected successfully.* Clicking the small x will dismiss this dialog box. The Project Builder should highlight: *Step 3*

[1] https://www.markdownguide.org/basic-syntax

Upload Dataset. Any mistakes made in the Create Task form can be edited later as described below.

6. Creating a Dataset

As a reminder, a LanguageARC data set is a manifest file enumerating the items for some task with either item specific test or media files for each item. For projects that only require citizen linguists to answer questions or respond to simple prompts via speech, text or controlled vocabulary, the dataset could be composed of only a manifest containing those questions or prompts with IDs. For tasks that require contributors to listen to speech, read text or view images or video, the dataset would include all of the media segmented into files the right size for individual items as well as the manifest file that lists them all, assigns them IDs and optionally adds text specific to the items.

Although it is relatively simple to modify the fields in the project and task forms, LanguageARC does not allow a project designer to change a data set. There is a research reason behind this design decision. A significant change to a data set may render the contributions made after the change incompatible with the contributions made before. LanguageARC cannot predict when a dataset change is significant (and one might argue that researchers often cannot predict either). To underscore the importance of a dataset on research outcomes, LanguageARC assigns a unique number to each data set, even (especially!) datasets used for the same task, and records any change in dataset ID in the task's report. The only way to modify the data available to a task is to upload a new data set, even if only trivially different from datasets uploaded previously. Also, because LanguageARC allows multiple tasks to use the same data set, uploading a new data set does not erase an old one. In fact, LanguageARC does not currently include a function for erasing data sets given their importance to research outcomes. Obviously then care is required in the definition of a dataset not only because uploading multiple copies of the same data wastes storage on LanguageARC servers but also importantly because dataset changes in the midst of an ongoing task could impact research outcomes in ways that are hard to predict.

Selecting *Upload Dataset.* should open *New Dataset* form. The Dataset Name must be globally unique and should be memorable to the project team. The Dataset Description should describe dataset contents and use. For the next field, the project designer will click the Browse button, browse local, or any locally attached, storage to find the manifest file and upload it. The same process applies to uploading any media files except that the project designer should select and upload all files in a single pass. The final question offers a one-time randomization of the dataset order. Otherwise the dataset is order as specified in the manifest. This decision interacts with ordering and assignment decisions made when building the task. For example, a researcher who wants to provide the items in the same order to all contributors (for example for some surveys) would select no randomization of the dataset and when building the task would again select no randomization and assignment within contributors. If each contributor is to see a unique randomization of the items, it is sufficient to choose randomization when building the task. Only when the form is complete, clicking the Save button will create the dataset. The familiar dialog box should appear saying: *Dataset created or selected successfully* and clicking the small x will dismiss it. If the dataset is very large in term of the number of size of files, creating the dataset may take longer than the previous steps.

7. Creating a Tool

To underscore the importance of tool design on research outcomes, LanguageARC assigns a unique number to each tool, records that change in a tool ID in the task's report and prohibits changes to a tool once created. The only way to change a tool is to first run a report to save all contributions made so far and then recreate the tool. As with dataset creation, care is required because any tool changes could impact the research outcomes in unpredictable ways.

With the project, task and dataset created, the project builder should have highlighted *Step 4: Create Tool*. The project designer should select Use Template to open the final Create Tool from Template form. There is a warning at the top that nothing is saved until the save button is clicked. Also, the project designer should not click Save until the form is complete. All fields on this form are new. The first asks for **exercise** specific text which can be thought of as instructions. They appear at the top of the tool and remain constant for all items in a task. A project can have multiple tasks each with different instructions but the instructions do not change within the task.

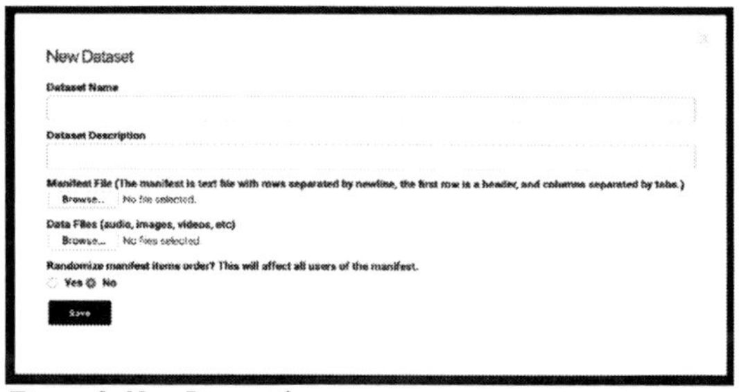

Figure 9: New Dataset form

The next field asks for the *Media Type*. The choice of text, audio, image, or video should match the type contained in the dataset. The 5th choice is labelled "manifest text" and indicates that there are no external media files and that all data for the task are included in the manifest. The third fields requires the project designer to select the column in which the media files are listed. Clicking on the arrow will pull down the list of the column headings in the manifest. If there are no media files any column can be selected.

Next, one decides whether the tool should offer a language selection. If the data and instructions make it clear that all tasks use a single language, then a language selector is not necessary. However, if the same activity can be done in multiple languages then 'yes' should be selected. A new field will appear indicating that there are two ways to add a language selector. The first is that the project designer can limit the range of languages to be selected by entering their names, each separated by a comma, in the text box. If the project designer chooses not to limit language selection, LanguageARC will load its universal language selector. This widget accepts all of the alternate names for all languages listed in the SIL Ethnologue. Each of these names indexes an official name and ISO code. The widget has look ahead so that as the user types the choices decrease. Because the number of language names in the SIL Ethnologue is immense and because many languages have similar names, it is best to use this widget only when the true number of languages for a task is too large to enumerate.

The next field requires the project designer to select the manifest column containing the item IDs in the dataset. This is important as the IDs will appear in the automatically created report as the link between citizen linguists contributions and the dataset.

The next two form fields allow the project designer to indicate whether manifest columns contain item specific text to be displayed. Selecting yes causes two additional fields to appear, the first for the column in the manifest containing the item specific text and the second asking what label should appear above that text. LanguageARC accommodates two columns of item specific text, the primary appearing directly above the secondary.

The next fields allow the project designer to decide how the users will respond to each item. The first permits the response as audio. The corresponding widget includes record, stop and re-do buttons. Three additional fields offer a level test (currently deactivated), level meter and playback button. All audio is once the contributor clicks the record button followed by the stop button. The re-do button makes additional recordings. Researchers should attend to report that indicates whether the audio was re-recorded and act accordingly.

The next allows the project designer to accept responses as text. If selected, two additional fields appear asking how to label the response in the report and in the tool. When text response is activated a simple textbox appears in the tool under the label specified.

The next field, Judgement Buttons, allows the project designer to accept responses as controlled vocabulary. One enters text for each choice, one per line. If that field is empty, the tool will add a submit button so contributors can indicate when they have completed an item. If choices are entered, the Multiple Choice field becomes relevant. If no is selected, the judgments will appear as buttons and each will have the effect of a submit. In other words if the contributor clicks any button that decision will be saved and the tool will move to the next item. If instead yes is selected the decisions will appear as checkboxes, the contributor will be able to select one or more and a separate Submit button will appear which the contributor must click when they have finished making their decision. Project designers can include any or all of response audio, response text and judgement button but this feature should be used carefully. Including too many response modes may confuse contributors and make the data difficult to analyze.

The last two fields are radio buttons asking if the tools should allow skipping and reporting bad items. Selecting yes to the first will cause a red skip button to appear in the tool that contributors can click if they do not know how, or prefer not to, respond to the item. Selecting yes for the second will cause a red button labeled Report to appear inside the tool that contributors can click to indicate that there is something wrong with the item for example the audio is missing. Only when the entire form is complete should the project designer click Save. If all has gone well a small dialog box should appear saying that the tool has been created. Clicking the small X will dismiss this dialog.

8. Reviewing and Editing Projects

Clicking the Project link in the LanguageARC menu opens the project grid that should now include the newly created project, which will be visible only to the project team initially, probably on the last page of entries. On the project main page and task list, *Edit* links will appear only for authorized project designers (see Figure 10). Clicking the *Edit* link beneath the project menu on the left of the Project Main Page or Task List opens the *Edit Project Details* forms while clicking the Edit link beneath any task title will open the *Edit Task Details* form. All of the fields will be familiar from the New Project and New Task forms with two exceptions. The Position field allows the project designer to enter a integer to order projects in the grid or the tasks on the task list. The Project Status and Task Status pull downs allows the designer to change status from *Prototype* to *Private* and to *Request Publication.* A *Private* project or task is one intended to be permanently accessible by invitation only, to a controlled group of contributors.

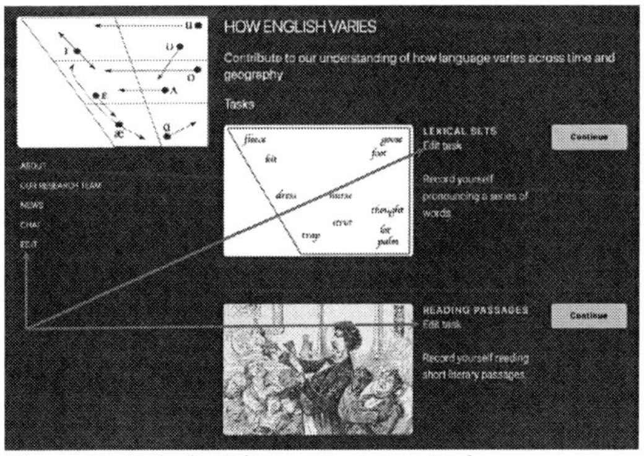

Figure 10: Links for Editing a Project or Task

To add Tasks to an existing project, an authorized project designer clicks the Create a Project link, but then selects *Choose an Existing Project* before selecting *Create New Task* and then continuing as described in §5 and following. It is possible to use an existing dataset in a new tasks if appropriate, for example to perform two different annotations over the same data in parallel. To do this the project designer would select *Choose Existing Dataset* rather than Upload Dataset at Step 3 in the Tool Builder. Although it is technically possible to upload a new data set for use with an existing task, given the interdependence of dataset and tool, this will require the task designer to Reset the Tool immediately after. This is not recommended for tasks in active use because of the possibility. Rather the task designer would be better served to prototype the new task and, when it is ready, invite users or request publication and then deactivate the old task by changing its status back to prototype. This will avoid confusing contributors and leaving the task in an undefined state and will keep the reports separate before and after the change.

9. Reporting

To report the results of a LanguageARC task, an authorized project designer clicks on their screen name in the upper right corner of any LanguageARC page. This opens the *Dashboard* as displayed in Figure 11. Clicking the Download Report button for the appropriate task will generate and download the report in TSV format in whatever way the browser is configured to accept it (e.g. save to a predefined folder, automatically open in a spreadsheet).

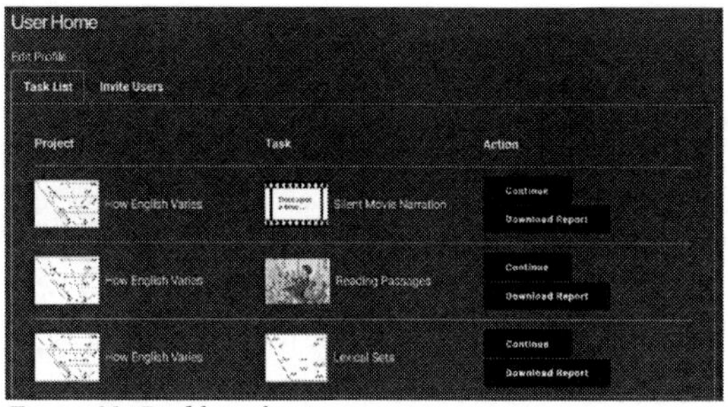

Figure 11: Dashboard

LanguageARC provides reports for every task using a consistent structure that begins with columns for the project ID and status, task ID and status, dataset ID, userID, country code and city from which the contribution was made followed by a date and time stamp using the GMT timezone. The remaining columns vary depending on the task. Figure 12 shows a tiny snippet of the report for a task to collect judgments of the home location of speakers based on their reading of an identical text, Chicken Little. The researcher who developed the project created multiple tasks to gather data on contributors' ability recognize the readers' social background and reports some of those results in this workshop (Cole 2020). Readers were from London, Surrey or Essex in the UK. Contributors could click a button to select one of those locations, skip the item, report it as bad (e.g. the audio was inaudible) or do nothing and simply exit the tool. The 11th and 12th columns contain the judgements contributed and the identifiers of the audio clips as the designer specified them in the manifest file. In the first **row** of the report snippet, the contributor exited the tool without making a judgment for clip 97. In the second, the contributor was offered audio clip 21 and clicked the Skip button. In the third row the contributor judged that the reader of clip 131 was from Essex.

Project ID	Project Status	Task ID	Task Status	Tool ID	Dataset ID	User ID	Country Code	City	Time	Judgment	Prompt ID
7	Published	24	Published	21	23	6	US	Fayetteville	2019-11-11 03:03:53 +0000		97
7	Published	24	Published	21	23	3	US	Philadelphia	2019-11-11 13:37:43 +0000	skipped	21
7	Published	24	Published	21	23	17	AU	Hobart	2019-12-03 12:41:48 +0000	Essex	131

Figure 12: A snippet of a LanguageARC report

One can also glean from the report that contributors come from diffuse locations, e.g. Philadelphia in the US and Hobart in Australia. This underscores the possibility that for a broadly available portal that tries to appeal to the public, there may be no time of day when a task is quiescent. It also shows that LanguageARC does not report locations any more specific than the city. This is to further protect the anonymity of contributors.

10. Conclusion

This paper has described to goal, features and operations of LanguageARC, a portal deigned to allow researchers to easily create projects and tasks that attract citizen linguists who are motivated by their interest in language and in the individual projects and by the opportunity to join with like-minded people, to learn about and make small contributions to those projects. This approach augments existing approaches that rely principally on monetary incentives to motivate contributions. By coordinating efforts that use these complementary approaches we will be able increase the number, scale and diversity of language resources in order to promote language related education, research and technology development.

11. Acknowledgements

LanguageARC is an outcome of the NIEUW project to investigate novel incentives and workflows in the elicitation of language data. Other NIEUW outcomes include the LingoBoingo.org language games portal and the language identification game, NameThatLanguage.org. The Linguistic Data Consortium and the University of Pennsylvania acknowledge the generous support of the US National Science Foundation via the Computer and Information Science and Engineering Directorate's Research Infrastructure program, grant 1730377.

12. Bibliographical References

Cieri, Christopher, Mark Liberman, Stephanie Strassel, Denise DiPersio, Jonathan Wright, Andrea Mazzucchi, James Fiumara (2018) From 'Solved Problems' to New Challenges: A Report on LDC Activities. In Calzolari, et. al., Proc. 11th International Conference on Language Resources and Evaluation (LREC 2018), pp. 3265-3269.

Christopher Cieri, James Fiumara, Mark Liberman, Chris Callison-Burch, Jonathan Wright (2018) Introducing NIEUW: Novel Incentives and Workflows for Eliciting Linguistic Data. In Calzolari, et. al., Proc. 11th International Conference on Language Resources and Evaluation (LREC 2018), pp. 151-155.

Cole, Amanda (2020) Identifications of Speaker Ethnicity in South-East England: Multicultural London English as a Divisible Perceptual Variety In Proceedings of the Citizen Linguistics for Language Resource Development workshop at LREC 2020.

Association for Computational Linguistics
209 N. Eighth Street
Stroudsburg, Pennsylvania 18360

ISBN 978-1-7138-1255-5

CURRAN ASSOCIATES INC.
proceedings
.com